JOHN O'DONOHUE

ANAM CARA

A BOOK OF CELTIC WISDOM

Cliff Street Books
An Imprint of HarperCollins*Publishers*

HarperCollins books may be purchased for educational, business, or sales promotional use. For information please write: Special Markets Department, HarperCollins Publishers, Inc., 10 East 53rd Street, New York, NY 10022.

FIRST EDITION

Designed by Ruth Lee

Library of Congress Cataloging-in-Publication Data

O'Donohue, John
    Anam ċara : a book of Celtic wisdom / John O'Donohue. — 1st ed.
        p.   cm.
    Includes bibliographical references.
    ISBN 0-06-018279-2
    1. Spiritual life.   2. Celts—Ireland—Religion.   3. Friendship—Religious aspects.   I. Title.
    BL624.O33   1997
    248'.089'9162—dc21   97-19212

97 98 99 00 01 ❖/RRD 10 9 8 7 6 5 4 3 2 1

BEANNACHT

For Josie

On the day when
the weight deadens
on your shoulders
and you stumble,
may the clay dance
to balance you.

And when your eyes
freeze behind
the gray window
and the ghost of loss
gets in to you,
may a flock of colors,
indigo, red, green
and azure blue
come to awaken in you
a meadow of delight.

When the canvas frays
in the curach of thought
and a stain of ocean
blackens beneath you,
may there come across the waters
a path of yellow moonlight
to bring you safely home.

May the nourishment of the earth be yours,
may the clarity of light be yours,
may the fluency of the ocean be yours,
may the protection of the ancestors be yours.

And so may a slow
wind work these words
of love around you,
an invisible cloak
to mind your life.

In memory of my father, Paddy O'Donohue,
who worked stone so poetically,
and my uncle Pete O'Donohue,
who loved the mountains

And my aunt Brigid

In memory of John, Willie, Mary,
and Ellie O'Donohue,
who emigrated and now rest in American soil

Contents

❧ CONTENTS ❧

❦ CONTENTS ❦

❦ CONTENTS ❦

❁ CONTENTS ❁

CONTENTS

ACKNOWLEDGMENTS

I wish to thank Diane Reverand, my editor at HarperCollins, for her encouragement and help; Kim Witherspoon and her agency for her belief in my work and its effective mediation; Tami Simon and Michael Taft at Sounds True for their care and support, and Anne Minogue for introducing me; John Devitt, who read the manuscript and offered a thorough, creative, and literary critique; Marian O'Beirn, who read each draft of the manuscript, for her encouragement, invaluable editorial advice, and attention; David Whyte for his brotherly care and generosity; Ellen Wingard for her support and confidence in the work; and my family for all the ordinary magic and laughter! To the landscape and the ancestors; *Do mo cáirde a tug foscad agus solas.*

Prologue

IT IS STRANGE TO BE HERE. THE MYSTERY NEVER LEAVES YOU alone. Behind your image, below your words, above your thoughts, the silence of another world waits. A world lives within you. No one else can bring you news of this inner world. Through the opening of the mouth, we bring out sounds from the mountain beneath the soul. These sounds are words. The world is full of words. There are so many talking all the time, loudly, quietly, in rooms, on streets, on television, on radio, in the paper, in books. The noise of words keeps what we call the world there for us. We take each other's sounds and make patterns, predictions, benedictions, and blasphemies. Each day, our tribe of language holds what we call the world together. Yet the uttering of the word reveals how each of us relentlessly creates. Everyone is an artist. Each person brings sound out of silence and coaxes the invisible to become visible.

Humans are new here. Above us, the galaxies dance out toward infinity. Under our feet is ancient earth. We are beautifully molded from this clay. Yet the smallest stone is millions of years older than us. In your thoughts, the silent universe seeks echo.

An unknown world aspires toward reflection. Words are the oblique mirrors that hold your thoughts. You gaze into these word-mirrors and catch glimpses of meaning, belonging, and shelter. Behind their bright surfaces is the dark and the silence. Words are like the god Janus, they face outward and inward at once.

If we become addicted to the external, our interiority will haunt us. We will become hungry with a hunger no image, person, or deed can still. To be wholesome, we must remain truthful to our vulnerable complexity. In order to keep our balance, we need to hold the interior and exterior, visible and invisible, known and unknown, temporal and eternal, ancient and new, together. No one else can undertake this task for you. You are the one and only threshold of an inner world. This wholesomeness is holiness. To be holy is to be natural, to befriend the worlds that come to balance in you. Behind the facade of image and distraction, each person is an artist in this primal and inescapable sense. Each one of us is doomed and privileged to be an inner artist who carries and shapes a unique world.

Human presence is a creative and turbulent sacrament, a

visible sign of invisible grace. Nowhere else is there such intimate and frightening access to the mysterium. Friendship is
the sweet grace that liberates us to approach, recognize, and
inhabit this adventure. This book is intended as an oblique
mirror in which you might come to glimpse the presence and
power of inner and outer friendship. Friendship is a creative
and subversive force. It claims that intimacy is the secret law
of life and universe. The human journey is a continuous act of
transfiguration. If approached in friendship, the unknown,
the anonymous, the negative, and the threatening gradually
yield their secret affinity with us. As an artist, the human
person is permanently active in this revelation. The imagination is the great friend of the unknown. Endlessly, it invokes
and releases the power of possibility. Friendship, then, is not
to be reduced to an exclusive or sentimental relationship; it is
a far more extensive and intensive force.

The Celtic mind was neither discursive nor systematic.
Yet in their lyrical speculation the Celts brought the sublime
unity of life and experience to expression. The Celtic mind
was not burdened by dualism. It did not separate what
belongs together. The Celtic imagination articulates the inner
friendship that embraces Nature, divinity, underworld, and
human world as one. The dualism that separates the visible
from the invisible, time from eternity, the human from the
divine, was totally alien to them. Their sense of ontological
friendship yielded a world of experience imbued with a rich

texture of otherness, ambivalence, symbolism, and imagination. For our sore and tormented separation, the possibility of this imaginative and unifying friendship is the Celtic gift.

The Celtic understanding of friendship finds its inspiration and culmination in the sublime notion of the *anam čara*. *Anam* is the Gaelic word for soul; *čara* is the word for friend. So *anam čara* means soul friend. The *anam čara* was a person to whom you could reveal the hidden intimacies of your life. This friendship was an act of recognition and belonging. When you had an *anam čara*, your friendship cut across all convention and category. You were joined in an ancient and eternal way with the friend of your soul. Taking this as our inspiration, we explore interpersonal friendship in chapter 1. Central here is the recognition and awakening of the ancient belonging between two friends. Since the birth of the human heart is an ongoing process, love is the continuous birth of creativity within and between us. We will explore longing as the presence of the divine and the soul as the house of belonging.

In chapter 2, we will outline a spirituality of friendship with the body. The body is your clay home, your only home in the universe. The body is in the soul; this recognition confers a sacred and mystical dignity on the body. The senses are divine thresholds. A spirituality of the senses is a spirituality of transfiguration. In chapter 3, we will explore the art of inner friendship. When you cease to fear your solitude, a new creativity awakens in you. Your forgotten or neglected inner wealth begins to reveal itself. You come home to yourself and learn to rest within. Thoughts are our inner senses. Infused with silence and solitude, they bring out the mystery of the inner landscape.

In chapter 4, we will reflect on work as a poetics of growth. The invisible hungers to become visible, to express itself in our actions. This is the inner desire of work. When our inner life can befriend the outer world of work, new imagination is awakened and great changes take place. In chapter 5, we will contemplate our friendship with the harvest time of life, old age. We will explore memory as the place where our vanished days secretly gather and acknowledge that the passionate heart never ages. Time is eternity living dangerously. In chapter 6, we will probe our necessary friendship with our original and ultimate companion, death. We will reflect on death as the invisible companion who walks the road of life with us from birth. Death is the great wound in the universe, the root of all fear and negativity. Friendship with our death enables us to celebrate the eternity of the soul, which death cannot touch.

The Celtic imagination loved the circle. It recognized how the rhythm of experience, nature, and divinity followed a circular pattern. In acknowledgment of this, the structure of this book follows a circular rhythm. It begins with a treatment of friendship as awakening, then explores the senses as immediate and creative thresholds. This builds the ground for a positive evaluation of solitude, which in turn seeks expression in the external world of work and action. As our outer energy diminishes, we are faced with the task of aging and dying. This structure follows the circle of life as it spirals toward death and attempts to illuminate the profound invitation it offers.

These chapters circle around a hidden, silent seventh chapter, which embraces the ancient namelessness at the heart of the human self. Here resides the unsayable, the ineffable. In essence, this book attempts a phenomenology of friendship in a lyrical-speculative form. It takes its inspiration from the implied and lyrical metaphysics of Celtic spirituality. Rather than being a piecemeal analysis of Celtic data, it attempts a somewhat broader reflection, an inner conversation with the Celtic imagination, endeavoring to thematize its implied philosophy and spirituality of friendship.

ONE

THE MYSTERY OF FRIENDSHIP

LIGHT IS GENEROUS

If you have ever had occasion to be out early in the morning before the dawn breaks, you will have noticed that the darkest time of night is immediately before dawn. The darkness deepens and becomes more anonymous. If you had never been to the world and never known what a day was, you couldn't possibly imagine how the darkness breaks, how the mystery and color of a new day arrive. Light is incredibly generous, but also gentle. When you attend to the way the dawn comes, you learn how light can coax the dark. The first fingers of light appear on the horizon, and ever so deftly and gradually, they pull the mantle of darkness away from the world. Quietly before you is the mystery of a new dawn, the new day.

Emerson said, "No one suspects the days to be Gods." It is one of the tragedies of modern culture that we have lost touch with these primal thresholds of nature. The urbanization of modern life has succeeded in exiling us from this fecund kinship with our mother earth. Fashioned from the earth, we are souls in clay form. We need to remain in rhythm with our inner clay voice and longing. Yet this voice is no longer audible in the modern world. We are not even aware of our loss, consequently, the pain of our spiritual exile is more intense in being largely unintelligible.

The world rests in the night. Trees, mountains, fields, and faces are released from the prison of shape and the burden of exposure. Each thing creeps back into its own nature within the shelter of the dark. Darkness is the ancient womb. Nighttime is womb-time. Our souls come out to play. The darkness absolves everything; the struggle for identity and impression falls away. We rest in the night. The dawn is a refreshing time, a time of possibility and promise. All the elements of nature—stones, fields, rivers, and animals—are suddenly there anew in the fresh dawn light. Just as darkness brings rest and release, so the dawn brings awakening and renewal. In our mediocrity and distraction, we forget that we are privileged to live in a wondrous universe. Each day, the dawn unveils the mystery of this universe. Dawn is the ultimate surprise; it awakens us to the immense "thereness" of nature. The wonderful subtle color of the universe arises to clothe everything. This is captured in a phrase from William Blake: "Colours are the wounds of light." Colors bring out the depth of secret presence at the heart of nature.

THE CELTIC CIRCLE OF BELONGING

All through Celtic poetry you find the color, power, and intensity of nature. How beautifully it recognizes the wind, the flowers, the breaking of the waves on the land. Celtic spirituality hallows the moon and adores the life force of the sun. Many of the ancient Celtic gods were close to the sources of fertility and belonging. Since the Celts were a nature people, the world of nature was both a presence and a companion. Nature nourished them; it was here that they felt their deepest belonging and affinity. Celtic nature poetry is suffused with this warmth, wonder, and belonging. One of the oldest Celtic prayers is a prayer called "St. Patrick's Breastplate"; its deeper name is "The Deer's Cry." There is no separation between subjectivity and the elements. Indeed, it is the very elemental forces that inform and elevate subjectivity:

> I arise today
> through the strength of heaven, light of sun,
> Radiance of moon,
> Splendor of fire,
> Speed of lightning,

Swiftness of wind,
Depth of sea,
Stability of earth,
Firmness of rock.

(TRANS. KUNO MEYER)

The Celtic world is full of immediacy and belonging. The Celtic mind adored the light. This is one of the reasons why Celtic spirituality is emerging as a new constellation in our times. We are lonely and lost in our hungry transparency. We desperately need a new and gentle light where the soul can shelter and reveal its ancient belonging. We need a light that has retained its kinship with the darkness. For we are sons and daughters of the darkness and of the light.

We are always on a journey from darkness into light. At first, we are children of the darkness. Your body and your face were formed first in the kind darkness of your mother's womb. Your birth was a first journey from darkness into light. All your life, your mind lives within the darkness of your body. Every thought that you have is a flint moment, a spark of light from your inner darkness. The miracle of thought is its presence in the night side of your soul; the brilliance of thought is born in darkness. Each day is a journey. We come out of the night into the day. All creativity awakens at this primal threshold where light and darkness test and bless each other. You only discover balance in your life when

4

you learn to trust the flow of this ancient rhythm. The year also is a journey with the same rhythm. The Celtic people had a deep sense of the circular nature of our journey. We come out of the darkness of winter into the possibility and effervescence of springtime.

Ultimately, light is the mother of life. Where there is no light, there can be no life. If the angle of the sun were to turn away from the earth, all human, animal, and vegetative life, as we know it, would disappear. Ice would freeze the earth again. Light is the secret presence of the divine. It keeps life awake. Light is a nurturing presence, which calls forth warmth and color in nature. The soul awakens and lives in light. It helps us to glimpse the sacred depths within us. Once human beings began to search for a meaning to life, light became one of the most powerful metaphors to express the eternity and depth of life. In the Western tradition, and indeed in the Celtic tradition, thought has often been compared to light. In its luminosity, the intellect was deemed to be the place of the divine within us.

When the human mind began to consider the next greatest mystery of life, the mystery of love, light was also always used as a metaphor for its power and presence. When love awakens in your life, in the night of your heart, it is like the dawn breaking within you. Where before there was anonymity, now there is intimacy; where before there was fear, now there is courage; where before in your life there was awkwardness, now there is a rhythm of grace and gracefulness; where before you used to be jagged, now you are elegant and in rhythm with your self. When love awakens in your life, it is like a rebirth, a new beginning.

THE HUMAN HEART IS NEVER COMPLETELY BORN

Though the human body is born complete in one moment, the birth of the human heart is an ongoing process. It is being birthed in every experience of your life. Everything that happens to you has the potential to deepen you. It brings to birth within you new territories of the heart. Patrick Kavanagh captures this sense of the benediction of happening: "Praise, praise, praise / The way it happened and the way it is." In the Christian tradition one of the most beautiful sacraments is baptism. It includes a special anointing of the baby's heart. Baptism comes from the Jewish tradition. For the Jewish people, the heart is the center of all the emotions. The heart is anointed as a main organ of the baby's health but also as the place where all its feelings will nest. The prayer intends that the new child will never become trapped, caught, or entangled in false inner networks of negativity, resentment, or destruction toward itself. The blessings also intend that the child will have a fluency of feeling in its life, that its feelings may flow freely and carry its soul out to the world and gather from the world delight and peace.

Against the infinity of the cosmos and the silent depths of

nature, the human face shines out as the icon of intimacy. It is here, in this icon of human presence, that divinity in creation comes nearest to itself. The human face is the icon of creation. Each person also has an inner face, which is always sensed but never seen. The heart is the inner face of your life. The human journey strives to make this inner face beautiful. It is here that love gathers within you. Love is absolutely vital for a human life. For love alone can awaken what is divine within you. In love, you grow and come home to your self. When you learn to love and to let your self be loved, you come home to the hearth of your own spirit. You are warm and sheltered. You are completely at one in the house of your own longing and belonging. In that growth and homecoming is the unlooked-for bonus in the act of loving another. Love begins with paying attention to others, with an act of gracious self-forgetting. This is the condition in which we grow.

Once the soul awakens, the search begins and you can never go back. From then on, you are inflamed with a special longing that will never again let you linger in the lowlands of complacency and partial fulfillment. The eternal makes you urgent. You are loath to let compromise or the threat of danger hold you back from striving toward the summit of fulfillment. When this spiritual path opens, you can bring an incredible generosity to the world and to the lives of others. Sometimes, it is easy to be generous outward, to give and give and give and yet remain ungenerous to yourself. You lose the balance of your soul if you are a generous giver but a mean receiver. You need to be generous to yourself in order to receive the love that surrounds you. You can suffer from a desperate hunger to be loved. You can search long years in lonely places, far outside yourself. Yet the whole time, this love is but a few inches away from you. It is at the edge of your soul, but you have been blind to its presence. Through some hurt, a door has slammed shut within the heart, and you are powerless to unlock it and receive the love. We must remain attentive in order to be able to receive. Boris Pasternak said, "When a great moment knocks on the door of your life, it is often no louder than the beating of your heart, and it is very easy to miss it."

It is strangely ironic that the world loves power and possessions. You can be very successful in this world, be admired by everyone, have endless possessions, a lovely family, success in your work, and have everything the world can give, but behind it all, you can be completely lost and miserable. If you have everything the world has to offer you, but you do not have love, then you are the poorest of the poorest of the poor. Every human heart hungers for love. If you do not have the warmth of love in your heart, there is no possibility of real celebration and enjoyment. No matter how hard, competent, self-assured, or respected you are, no matter what you think of yourself or what others think of you, the one thing you deeply long for is love. No matter where we are, who we are, what we are, or what kind of journey we are on, we all need love.

In his *Ethics*, Aristotle devotes several chapters to reflection on friendship. He grounds friendship on the idea of goodness and beauty. A friend is someone who wishes what is good for the other. Aristotle acknowledges how in the complexity of individuality, interiority is mirrored and fulfilled in the discovery and activity of friendship: "Our feelings towards our friends reflect our feelings towards ourselves." He acknowledges the patience required to develop real friendship: "The wish for friendship develops rapidly, but friendship does not." Friendship is the grace that warms and sweetens our lives: "Nobody would choose to live without friends even if he had all other good things."

LOVE IS THE NATURE OF THE SOUL

The soul needs love as urgently as the body needs air. In the warmth of love, the soul can be itself. All the possibilities of your human destiny are asleep in your soul. You are here to realize and honor these possibilities. When love comes in to your life, unrecognized dimensions of your destiny awaken and blossom and grow. Possibility is the secret heart of time. On its outer surface time is vulnerable to transience. Regardless of its sadness or beauty, each day empties and vanishes. In its deeper heart, time is transfiguration. Time minds possibility and makes sure that nothing is lost or forgotten. That which seems to pass away on the surface of time is in fact transfigured and housed in the tabernacle of memory. Possibility is the secret heart of creativity. Martin Heidegger speaks about the "ontological priority" of possibility. At the deepest level of being, possibility is both mother and transfigured destination of what we call events and facts. This quiet and secret world of the eternal is the soul. Love is the nature of the soul. When we love and allow ourselves to be loved, we begin more and more to inhabit the kingdom of the eternal. Fear changes into courage, emptiness becomes plenitude, and distance becomes intimacy.

The *anam-čara* experience opens a friendship that is not wounded or limited by separation or distance. Such friendship can remain alive even when the friends live far away from each other. Because they have broken through the barriers of persona and egoism to the soul level, the unity of their souls is not easily severed. When the soul is awakened, physical space is transfigured. Even across the distance, two friends can stay attuned to each other and continue to sense the flow of each other's lives. With your *anam čara* you awaken the eternal. In this soul-space, there is no distance. This is beautifully illustrated during the meal in the film *Babette's Feast* where an old soldier speaks to the woman he loved from youth but was not allowed to marry. He tells her that even though he hadn't seen her since, she had been always at his side.

Love is our deepest nature, and consciously or unconsciously, each of us searches for love. We often choose such false ways to satisfy this deep hunger. An excessive concentration on our work, achievements, or spiritual quest can actually lead us away from the presence of love. In the work of soul, our false urgency can utterly mislead us. We do not need to go out to find love; rather, we need to be still and let love discover us. Some of the most beautiful writing on love is in the Bible. Paul's letter to the Corinthians is absolutely beautiful. There he writes, "Love is always patient and kind; love is never boastful or conceited; it is never rude or selfish; it does not take offense, and is not resentful. . . . Love is always ready to excuse, to trust, to hope and to endure whatever comes." Elsewhere the Bible says, "Perfect love casts out all fear."

THE *UMBRA NIHILI*

In a vast universe that often seems sinister and unaware of us, we need the presence and shelter of love to transfigure our loneliness. This cosmic loneliness is the root of all inner loneliness. All of our life, everything we do, think, and feel is surrounded by nothingness. Hence we become afraid so easily. The fourteenth-century mystic Meister Eckhart says that all of human life stands under the shadow of nothingness, the *umbra nihili*. Nevertheless, love is the sister of the soul. Love is the deepest language and presence of soul. In and through the warmth and creativity of love, the soul shelters us from the

bleakness of that nothingness. We cannot fill up our emptiness with objects, possessions, or people. We have to go deeper
into that emptiness; then we will find beneath nothingness
the flame of love waiting to warm us.

No one can hurt you as deeply as the one you love. When
you allow the Other inside your life, you leave yourself open.
Even after years together, your affection and trust can be disappointed. Life is dangerously unpredictable. People change,
often quite dramatically and suddenly. Bitterness and resentment quickly replace belonging and affection. Every friendship travels at sometime through the black valley of despair.
This tests every aspect of your affection. You lose the attraction and the magic. Your sense of each other darkens and your
presence is sore. If you can come through this time, it can
purify your love, and falsity and need will fall away. It will
bring you onto new ground where affection can grow again.

Sometimes a friendship turns, and the partners fix on each
other at their points of mutual negativity. When you meet
only at the point of poverty between you, it is as if you give
birth to a ghost who would devour every shred of your affection. Your essence is rifled. You become helpless and repetitive with each other. Here you need deep prayer and great vig-
ilance and care in order to redirect your souls. Love can hurt us
deeply. We need to take great care. The blade of nothingness
cuts deeply. Others want to love, to give themselves, but they
have no energy. They carry around in their hearts the corpses

of past relationships and are addicted to hurt as confirmation of identity. Where a friendship recognizes itself as a gift, it will remain open to its own ground of blessing.

When you love, you open your life to an Other. All your barriers are down. Your protective distances collapse. This person is given absolute permission to come into the deepest temple of your spirit. Your presence and life can become this person's ground. It takes great courage to let someone so close. Since the body is in the soul, when you let someone so near, you let the person become part of you. In the sacred kinship of real love two souls are twinned. The outer shell and contour of identity become porous. You suffuse each other.

THE *ANAM ĊARA*

In the Celtic tradition, there is a beautiful understanding of love and friendship. One of the fascinating ideas here is the idea of soul-love; the old Gaelic term for this is *anam ċara*. *Anam* is the Gaelic word for soul and *ċara* is the word for friend. So *anam ċara* in the Celtic world was the "soul friend." In the early Celtic church, a person who acted as a teacher, companion, or spiritual guide was called an *anam ċara*. It originally referred to someone to whom you confessed, revealing the hidden intimacies of your life. With the *anam ċara* you could share your innermost self, your mind and your heart. This friendship was an act of recognition and belonging. When you had an *anam ċara*, your friendship cut across all convention, morality, and category. You were joined in an ancient and eternal way with the "friend of your soul." The Celtic understanding did not set limitations of space or time on the soul. There is no cage for the soul. The soul is a divine light that flows into you and into your Other. This art of belonging awakened and fostered a deep and special companionship. In his *Conferences*, John Cassian says this bond between friends is indissoluble: "This, I say, is what is broken by no chances, what no interval of time or space can sever or destroy, and what even death itself cannot part."

In everyone's life, there is great need for an *anam čara*, a soul friend. In this love, you are understood as you are without mask or pretension. The superficial and functional lies and half-truths of social acquaintance fall away, you can be as you really are. Love allows understanding to dawn, and understanding is precious. Where you are understood, you are at home. Understanding nourishes belonging. When you really feel understood, you feel free to release yourself into the trust and shelter of the other person's soul. This recognition is described in a beautiful line from Pablo Neruda: "You are like nobody since I love you." This art of love discloses the special and sacred identity of the other person. Love is the only light that can truly read the secret signature of the other person's individuality and soul. Love alone is literate in the world of origin; it can decipher identity and destiny.

It is precisely in awakening and exploring this rich and

opaque inner landscape that the *anam-cara* experience illuminates the mystery and kindness of the divine. The *anam cara* is
God's gift. Friendship is the nature of God. The Christian
concept of god as Trinity is the most sublime articulation of
otherness and intimacy, an eternal interflow of friendship.
This perspective discloses the beautiful fulfillment of our
immortal longing in the words of Jesus, who said, Behold, I
call you friends. Jesus, as the son of God, is the first Other
in the universe; he is the prism of all difference. He is the
secret *anam cara* of every individual. In friendship with him,
we enter the tender beauty and affection of the Trinity. In
the embrace of this eternal friendship, we dare to be free.
There is a beautiful Trinitarian motif running through Celtic
spirituality. This little invocation captures this:

The Sacred Three
My fortress be
Encircling me
Come and be round
My hearth and my home.

Consequently, love is anything but sentimental. In fact, it
is the most real and creative form of human presence. Love is
the threshold where divine and human presence ebb and flow
into each other.

All presence depends on consciousness. Where there is a

depth of awareness, there is a reverence for presence. Where consciousness is dulled, distant, or blind, the presence grows faint and vanishes. Consequently, awareness is one of the greatest gifts you can bring to your friendship. Many people have an *anam čara* of whom they are not truly aware. Their lack of awareness cloaks the friend's presence and causes feelings of distance and absence. Sadly, it is often loss that awakens presence, by then it is too late. It is wise to pray for the grace of recognition. Inspired by awareness, you may then discover beside you the *anam čara* of whom your longing has always dreamed.

The Celtic tradition recognized that an *anam-čara* friendship was graced with affection. Friendship awakens affection. The heart learns a new art of feeling. Such friendship is neither cerebral nor abstract. In Celtic tradition, the *anam čara* was not merely a metaphor or ideal. It was a soul-bond that existed as a recognized and admired social construct. It altered the meaning of identity and perception. When your affection is kindled, the world of your intellect takes on a new tenderness and compassion. The *anam čara* brings epistemological integration and healing. You look and see and understand differently. Initially, this can be disruptive and awkward, but it gradually refines your sensibility and transforms your way of being in the world. Most fundamentalism, greed, violence, and oppression can be traced back to the separation of idea and affection. For too long we have been blind to the cognitive riches of feeling and the affective depth of ideas. Aristotle said in *De Anima*, "Perception is ex hypothesi a form of affection and being moved; and the same goes for thinking and knowing. . . . Thinking particularly is like a peculiar affection of the soul." The *anam-ċara* perspective is sublime because it permits us to enter this unity of ancient belonging.

INTIMACY AS SACRED

In our culture, there is an excessive concentration on the notion of relationship. People talk incessantly about relationships. It is a constant theme on television, film, and in the media. Technology and media are not uniting the world. They pretend to provide a world that is internetted, but in reality, all they deliver is a simulated world of shadows. Accordingly, they make our human world more anonymous and lonely. In a world where the computer replaces human encounter and psychology replaces religion, it is no wonder that there is an obsession with relationship. Unfortunately, however, "relationship" has become an empty center around which our lonely hunger forages for warmth and belonging. Much of the public language of intimacy is hollow, and its incessant repetition only betrays the complete absence of intimacy. Real intimacy is a sacred experience. It never exposes its secret trust and belonging to the voyeuristic eye of a neon culture. Real intimacy is of the soul, and the soul is reserved.

The Bible says that no one can see God and live. In a transferred sense, no person can see himself and live. All you can ever achieve is a sense of your soul. You gain little glimpses of its light, colors, and contours. You feel the inspiration of its possibilities and the wonder of its mysteries. In the Celtic tradition, and especially in the Gaelic language, there is a refined sense of the sacredness that the approach to another person should embody. The word *hello* does not exist in Gaelic. The way that you encounter someone is through blessing. You say, *Dia Dhuit*, God be with you. They respond, *Dia is Muire dhuit*, God and Mary be with you. When you are leaving a person, you say, *Go gcumhdaí Dia thu*, May God come to your assistance or *Go gcoinne Dia thú*, May God keep you. The ritual of encounter is framed at the beginning and at the end with blessing. Regularly throughout conversation in Gaelic, there is explicit recognition that the divine is present in others. This presence is also recognized and embodied in old sayings such as, "the hand of the stranger is the hand of God." The stranger does not come accidentally; he brings a particular gift and illumination.

THE MYSTERY OF APPROACH

For years I have had an idea for a short story about a world where you would approach only one person in the course of your life. Naturally, one would have to subtract biological considerations from this assumption in order to draw this imaginary world. You would have to practice years of silence before the mystery of presence in the Other, then you could begin to approach. In the course of your life, you might approach only one or two people. This idea gains in reality if you view your life carefully and distinguish between acquaintances and friends. A friend is different from an acquaintance. Friendship is a deeper and more sacred connection. Shakespeare has a beautiful phrase for this: "The friends thou hast and their attention tried, grapple them to your soul with hoops of steel." So a friend is incredibly precious. A friend is a loved one who awakens your life in order to free the wild possibilities within you.

Ireland is a land of many ruins. Ruins are not empty. They are sacred places full of presence. A friend of mine, a priest in Connemara, was going to build a parking lot outside his church. There was a ruin nearby that had been vacated for fifty or sixty years. He went to the man whose family had lived there long ago and asked the man to give him the stones for the foundation. The man refused. The priest asked why, and the man said, *"Céard a dhéanfadh anamacha mo mhuinitíre ansin?"*—that is, "What would the souls of my ancestors do then?" The implication was that even in this ruin long since vacated, the souls of those who had once lived there still had a particular affinity and attachment to this place. The life and passion of a person leave an imprint on the ether of a place. Love does not remain within the heart, it flows out to build secret tabernacles in a landscape.

DIARMUID AND GRÁINNE

Traveling throughout Ireland, you will see beautiful stone shapes called dolmens. A dolmen is two massive, long tables of limestone, laid down parallel to each other. Over them as a kind of shelter is placed another giant capstone. In the Celtic tradition these were known as *Leaba Dhiarmada agus Gráinne*; that is, the bed of Diarmuid and Gráinne. The legend tells that Gráinne was to marry Fionn, chief of the Fianna, the old Celtic warriors. She fell in love with Diarmuid and threatened him with magical destruction if he refused to elope with her. The two of them eloped, and the Fianna chased them all over Ireland. They were cared for by the animals and received advice from wise people on how to evade their pursuers. They were told, for instance, not to spend more than two nights in any one place. But it was said that when they rested at night, Diarmuid put up the dolmen as a shelter for his lover. The actual archaeological evidence shows that these were burial places. The legend is more interesting and resonant. It is a lovely image of the helplessness that sometimes accompanies love. When you fall in love, common sense, rationality, and your normal serious, reserved, and respectable persona dissolve. Suddenly you are like an adolescent again; there is new fire in your life. You become revitalized. Where there is no passion, your soul is either asleep or absent. When your passion awakens, your soul becomes young and free and dances again. In this old Celtic legend, we see the power of love and the energy of passion. One of the most powerful poems about how this longing transfigures life is by Goethe and is called "Blessed Longing."

Tell no one else, only the wise
For the crowd will sneer at one
I wish to praise what is fully alive,
What longs to flame toward death.

When the calm enfolds the love-nights
That created you, where you have created
A feeling from the Unkown steals over you
While the tranquil candle burns.

You remain no longer caught
In the peneumbral gloom
You are stirred and new, you desire
To soar to higher creativity.

No distance makes you ambivalent.
You come on wings, enchanted
In such hunger for light, you
Become the butterfly burnt to nothing.

So long as you have not lived this:
To die is to become new,

You remain a gloomy guest
On the dark earth.

(TRANS. BY THE AUTHOR)

This poem captures the wonderful spiritual force at the heart of longing. It suggests that true vitality is hidden within longing. When you give in to creative passion, it will bring you to the ultimate thresholds of transfiguration and renewal. This growth causes pain, but it is a sacred pain. It would be much more tragic to have cautiously avoided these depths and remained marooned on the shiny surfaces of the banal.

LOVE AS ANCIENT RECOGNITION

Real friendship or love is not manufactured or achieved by an act of will or intention. Friendship is always an act of recognition. This metaphor of friendship can be grounded in the clay nature of the human body. When you find the person you love, an act of ancient recognition brings you together. It is as if millions of years before the silence of nature broke, your lover's clay and your clay lay side by side. Then in the turning of the seasons, your one clay divided and separated. You began to rise as distinct clay forms, each housing a different individuality and destiny. Without even knowing it, your secret memory mourned your loss of each other. While your clay selves wandered for thousands of years through the universe, your longing for each other never faded. This metaphor helps to explain how in the moment of friendship two souls suddenly recognize each other. It could be a meeting on the street, or at a party or a lecture, or just a simple, banal introduction, then suddenly there is the flash of recognition and the embers of kinship glow. There is an awakening between you, a sense of ancient knowing. Love opens the door of ancient recognition. You enter. You come home to each other at last. As Euripides said, "Two friends, one soul."

In the classical tradition, this is wonderfully expressed in the *Symposium*, Plato's magical dialogue on the nature of love. Plato adverts to the myth that humans in the beginning were not single individuals. Each person was two selves in one. Then they became separated; consequently, you spend your life looking for your other half. When you find and discover each other, it is through this act of profound recognition. In friendship, an ancient circle closes. That which is ancient between you will mind you, shelter you, and hold you together. When two people fall in love, each comes in out of the loneliness of exile, home to the one house of belonging. At weddings, it is appropriate to acknowledge the gracious destiny that enabled this couple to recognize each other when they met. Each recognized the other as the one in whom their heart could be at home. Love should never be a burden, for there is more between you than your mutual presence.

THE CIRCLE OF BELONGING

We need more resonant words to mirror this than the tired word *relationship*. Phrases like "an ancient circle closes" or "an ancient belonging awakens and discovers itself" help to bring out the deeper meaning and mystery of encounter. This is the more sacred language of the soul for togetherness and intimacy. When two people love each other, there is a third force between them. Sometimes when a friendship is in trouble, it is not to be healed by endless analysis or counseling. You need to change the rhythm of seeing each other and come in contact again with the ancient belonging that brought you together. If you invoke its power and presence around you, this ancient affinity will hold you together. Two people who are really awakened inhabit the one circle of belonging. They have awakened a more ancient force around them that will hold them together and mind them.

Friendship needs a lot of nurturing. Often people devote their primary attention to the facts of their lives, to their situation, to their work, to their status. Most of their energy goes into doing. Meister Eckhart writes beautifully about this temptation. He says many people wonder where they should be and what they should do, when in fact they should be more concerned about how to be. The love side of your life is the place of greatest tenderness within you. In a culture preoccupied with fixities and definites and correspondingly impatient of mystery, it is difficult to step out from the transparency of false light into the more candlelit world of the soul. Perhaps the light of the soul is like Rembrandt's light—that tawny, gold light for which Rembrandt's work is known. This light gives you such a real sense of the depth and substance of the figures on whom it gently shines. It achieves a profound complexity of presence through the subtle use of shadow. Such golden earth-light is the natural sister of shadow and cradle of illumination.

THE *KALYANA-MITRA*

The Buddhist tradition has a lovely concept of friendship, the notion of the *Kalyana-mitra*, the "noble friend." Your *Kalyana-mitra*, your noble friend, will not accept pretension but will gently and very firmly confront you with your own blindness. No one can see his life totally. As there is a blind spot in the retina of the human eye, there is also in the soul a blind side where you are not able to see. Therefore you must depend on the one you love to see for you what you cannot see for yourself. Your *Kalyana-mitra* complements your vision in a kind and critical way. Such friendship is creative and critical; it is willing to negotiate awkward and uneven territories of contradiction and woundedness.

One of the deepest longings of the human soul is the longing to be seen. In an ancient myth Narcissus looks into the pool, sees his own face, and becomes obsessed with it. Unfortunately, there is no mirror in the world where you can catch a glimpse of your soul. You cannot even see your own body completely. If you look behind you, the front of your body is out of view. You can never be fully visually present to your self. The one you love, your *anam čara*, your soul friend, is the truest mirror to reflect your soul. The honesty and clarity of true friendship also brings out the real contour of your spirit. It is beautiful to have such a presence in your life.

THE SOUL AS DIVINE ECHO

We are capable of such love and belonging because the soul holds the echo of a primal intimacy. When talking about primal things, the Germans talk of *ursprüngliche Dinge*—original things. There is an *Ur-Intimität in der Seele;* that is, a primal intimacy in the soul; this original echo whispers within every heart. The soul did not invent itself. It is a presence from the divine world, where intimacy has no limit or barrier.

You can never love another person unless you are equally involved in the beautiful but difficult spiritual work of learning to love yourself. There is within each of us, at the soul level, an enriching fountain of love. In other words, you do not have to go outside yourself to know what love is. This is not selfishness, and it is not narcissism; they are negative obsessions with the need to be loved. Rather this is the wellspring of love within the heart.

Through their need for love, people who lead solitary lives often stumble upon this great fountain. They learn to whisper awake the deep well of love within. This is not a question of forcing yourself to love yourself. It is more a question of exercising reserve, of inviting the wellspring of love that is, after all, your deepest nature to flow through your life. When this happens, the ground that has hardened within you grows soft again. Through a lack of love everything hardens. There is nothing as lonely in the world as that which has hardened or grown cold. Bitterness and coldness are the ultimate defeat.

If you find that your heart has hardened, one of the gifts that you should give yourself is the gift of the inner wellspring. You should invite this inner fountain to free itself. You can work on yourself in order to unsilt this, so that gradually the nourishing waters begin in a lovely osmosis to infuse and pervade the hardened clay of your heart. Then the miracle of love happens within you. Where before there was hard, bleak, unyielding, dead ground, now there is growth, color, enrichment, and life flowing from the lovely wellspring of love. This is one of the most creative approaches in transfiguring what is negative within us. You are sent here to learn to love and to receive love. The greatest gift new love brings into your life is the awakening to the hidden love within. This makes you independent. You are now able to come close to the other, not out of need or with the wearying apparatus of projection, but out of genuine intimacy, affinity, and belonging. It is a freedom. Love

should make you free. You become free of the hungry, blister-
ing need with which you continually reach out to scrape affir-
mation, respect, and significance for yourself from things and
people outside yourself. To be holy is to be home, to be able to
rest in the house of belonging that we call the soul.

THE WELLSPRING OF LOVE WITHIN

You can search far and in hungry places for love. It is a great
consolation to know that there is a wellspring of love within
yourself. If you trust that this wellspring is there, you will then
be able to invite it to awaken. The following exercise could
help develop awareness of this capacity. When you have
moments on your own or spaces in your time, just focus on the
well at the root of your soul. Imagine that nourishing stream of
belonging, ease, peace, and delight. Feel, with your visual
imagination, the refreshing waters of that well gradually flowing up through the arid earth of the neglected side of your
heart. It is helpful to imagine this particularly before you sleep.
Then during the night you will be in a constant flow of enrichment and belonging. You will find that when you awake at
dawn, there will be a lovely, quiet happiness in your spirit.

One of the most precious things you should always preserve in a friendship and in love is your own difference. It can
happen within the circle of love that one person will tend to
imitate the other or reimagine himself in the image of the

other. While this may indicate a desire for total commitment, it is also destructive and dangerous. There was an old man I knew on an island off the West of Ireland. He had an unusual hobby. He used to collect photographs of newly married couples. He would then get a photograph of that couple some ten years later. From this second photograph, he would begin to demonstrate how one member of the couple was beginning to resemble the other. Often in a relationship there can be a subtle homogenizing force, which is destructive. The irony is that it is usually the difference between people that makes one person attractive to another. Consequently, this difference needs to be preserved and nurtured.

Love is also a force of light and nurture that liberates you to inhabit to the full your own difference. There should be no imitation of each other; no need to be defensive or protective in each other's presence. Love should encourage and free you fully into your full potential.

In order to preserve your own difference in love, you need plenty of room for your soul. It is interesting that in Hebrew one of the original words for salvation is also the word for space. If you were born on a farm, you realize that space is vital, especially when you are sowing something. If you plant two trees side by side, they will smother each other. That which grows needs space. Kahlil Gibran says, "Let there be spaces in your togetherness. Let the winds of the heavens dance between you." Space allows your otherness to find its own rhythm and contour. Yeats speaks of "a little space for the rose breath to fill." One of the lovely areas of love where space can be rendered beautiful is when two people make love. The one you love is the one to whom you can bring the full array and possibility and delight of your senses in the knowledge that they will be received in welcome and tenderness. Since the body is in the soul, the body is illuminated all around with soul-light. It is suffused with a gentle, sacred light. Making love with someone should not be merely a physical or mechanical release. It should engage the spiritual depth that awakens when you enter the soul of another person.

The soul of a person is most intimate. You meet a person's soul before you meet that person's body. When you meet soul and body as one, you enter the world of the Other. If a person could bring a gentle and reverent recognition to the depth and beauty of that encounter, it would extend incredible possibilities of delight and ecstasy within love-making. It would free in both people this inner wellspring of deeper love. It would reunite them externally with this third force of light, the ancient circle, that actually brings the two souls together in the first place.

THE TRANSFIGURATION OF THE SENSES

The mystics are among the most trustable in this area of sensuous love, and they have a lovely theology of the sensuous implicit in their writings. The mystics never preach a denial of the senses, rather they speak of the transfiguration of the senses. They recognize that there is a certain gravity or darkness in Eros that can sometimes predominate. The light of the soul can transfigure this tendency and bring balance and poise. The beauty of such mystical reflection on Eros reminds us that Eros is ultimately the energy of divine creativity. In the transfiguration of the sensuous, the wildness of eros and the playfulness of the soul come into lyrical rhythm.

Modern Ireland has had a complex and painful journey toward the recognition and acceptance of Eros. In the old Irish tradition, there was a wonderfully vibrant acknowledgment of the power of Eros and erotic love. This finds expression in one of the most interesting poems from that era, a poem by Brian Merriman called *"Cúirt an Mheáin Oidhce"* or "The Midnight Court." Written in the eighteenth century, much of this poem is given from the perspective of a woman. It is a radically free, feminist perception. The woman's voice speaks:

Amn't I plump and sound as a bell,
Lips for kissing, and teeth for smiling,
Blossomy skin and forehead shining,
My eyes are blue and my hair is thick
and coils and streams about my neck;
A man who's looking for a wife

Here's a face that will keep for life;
Hand and arm and neck and breast
Each is better than the rest;
Look at that waist! My legs are long
Limber as willows and light and strong.

(TRANS. BY FRANK O'CONNOR)

This very long poem is a ribald celebration of the erotic. There is no intrusion of the frequently negative language of morality, which tries to separate sexuality into pure and impure. It is redundant in any case to use such words about clay creatures. How could you possibly have such purity in a clay creature? A clay creature is always a mixture of light and darkness. The beauty of Eros is its passionate thresholds where light and darkness meet within the person. We need to reimagine God as the energy of transfigurative Eros, the source from which all creativity flows.

Pablo Neruda has written some of the most beautiful love lines. He says, "I will bring you happy flowers from the mountains, bluebells, / dark hazels, and rustic baskets of kisses. / I want / to do with you what Spring does with the cherry trees." This thought is so beautiful; it shows that love is also the awakening of springtime in the clay part of the heart. Yeats, too, wrote some inspiring lines of love poetry, such as "But one man loved the pilgrim soul in you / and loved the sorrows of your changing face." These poems show a recognition of the special depth and presence within the beloved. Love helps you to see the Other in his or her own unique and special nature.

THE WOUNDED GIFT

One of the great powers of love is balance; it helps us move toward transfiguration. When two people come together, an ancient circle closes between them. They also come to each other not with empty hands, but with hands full of gifts for each other. Often these are wounded gifts; this awakens the dimension of healing within love. When you really love someone, you shine the light of your soul on the beloved. We know from nature that sunlight brings everything to growth. If you look at flowers early on a spring morning, they are all closed. When the light of the sun catches them, they trustingly open out and give themselves to the new light.

When you love someone who is very hurt, one of the worst things you can do is to directly address the hurt and make an issue out of it. A strange dynamic comes alive in the soul if you make something into an issue. It becomes a habit and keeps recurring in a pattern. Frequently, it is better simply to acknowledge that there is a wound there, but then stay away from it. Every chance you get, shine the gentle light of the soul in on the wound. It is helpful to remember that there are ancient resources of renewal and refreshment in the circle

of love that bring and hold you both together. The destiny of
your love is never dependent merely on the fragile resources of
your separate subjectivities. You can invoke the healing of the
third force of light between you; this can bring forgiveness,
consolation, and healing in stony times.

When you love someone, it is destructive to keep scraping at the clay of your belonging. There is much to recom-
mend not interfering with your love. Two people who love
each other should never feel called to explain to an outside
party why they love each other, or why it is that they belong
together. The place that they belong is a secret place. Their
souls know why they are together; and they should trust that
togetherness. If you keep interfering with your connection
with your Other, your lover, your *anam čara*, you gradually
begin to force a distance between you. There is this wonderful two-line poem from Thom Gunn called "Jamesian."
Henry James is the most precise and utterly nuanced of nov-
elists. He described things in such fine detail and from so
many different angles. But such insidious analysis can
become obsessive and destructive of the lyrical presence of
love.

JAMESIAN

Their relationship consisted
in discussing if it existed.

If you keep shining the neon light of analysis and accountability on the tender tissue of your belonging, you make it parched and barren.

A person should always offer a prayer of graciousness for the love that has awakened in them. When you feel love for your beloved and the beloved's love for you, now and again you should offer the warmth of your love as a blessing for those who are damaged and unloved. Send that love out into the world to people who are desperate, to those who are starving, to those who are trapped in prison, in hospitals, and into all the brutal terrains of bleak and tormented lives. When you send that love out from the bountifulness of your own love, it reaches other people. This love is the deepest power of prayer.

IN THE KINGDOM OF LOVE, THERE IS NO COMPETITION

Prayer is the act and presence of sending this light from the bountifulness of your love to other people to heal, free, and bless them. When there is love in your life, you should share it spiritually with those who are pushed to the very edge of life. There is a lovely idea in the Celtic tradition that if you send out goodness from yourself, or if you share that which is happy or good within you, it will all come back to you multiplied ten thousand times. In the kingdom of love there is no competition; there is no possessiveness or control. The more love you give away, the more love you will have. One remembers here Dante's notion that the secret rhythm of the universe is the rhythm of love, which moves the stars and the planets. Love is the source, center, and destiny of experience.

A Friendship Blessing

May you be blessed with good friends.
May you learn to be a good friend to yourself.
May you be able to journey to that place in your soul where
    there is great love, warmth, feeling, and forgiveness.
May this change you.
May it transfigure that which is negative, distant, or cold
    in you.
May you be brought in to the real passion, kinship, and
    affinity of belonging.
May you treasure your friends.
May you be good to them and may you be there for them;
    may they bring you all the blessings, challenges, truth,
    and light that you need for your journey.
May you never be isolated.
May you always be in the gentle nest of belonging with your
    anam čara.

TWO

TOWARD A SPIRITUALITY
OF THE SENSES

THE FACE IS THE ICON OF CREATION

Landscape is the firstborn of creation. It was here hundreds of millions of years before the flowers, the animals, or the people appeared. Landscape was here on its own. It is the most ancient presence in the world, though it needs a human presence to acknowledge it. One could imagine that the oceans went silent and the winds became still the first time the human face appeared on earth; it is the most amazing thing in creation. In the human face, the anonymity of the universe becomes intimate. The dream of the winds and the oceans, the silence of the stars and the mountains, reached a mother-presence in the face. The hidden, secret warmth of creation comes to expression here. The face is the icon of creation. In the human mind, the universe first becomes resonant with itself. The face is the mirror of the mind. In the human person creation finds the intimacy it mutely craves. Within the mirror of the mind it becomes possible for diffuse and endless nature to behold itself.

The human face is an artistic achievement. On such a small surface an incredible variety and intensity of presence can be expressed. This breadth of presence overflows the limitation of the physical form. No two faces are exactly the same. There is always a special variation of presence in each one. Each face is a particular intensity of human presence. When you love someone and are separated from them for a long time, it is lovely to receive a letter or a phone call or even, in the silence of your own spirit, to sense their presence. Yet there is such deeper excitement when you return again and see the face you love; at this moment you enjoy a feast of seeing. In that face, you see the intensity and depth of loving presence looking toward you and meeting you. It is beautiful to see each other again. In Africa certain forms of greeting mean, "I see you." In Connemara, the phrase used to describe popularity and admiration is, *"Tá agaidh an phobail ort"*—that is, "The face of the people is toward you."

When you live in the silence and solitude of the land, cities seem startling. In cities, there are such an incredible number of faces: the faces of strangers moving all the time with rapidity and intensity. When you look at their faces, you see the particular intimacy of their lives imaged. In a certain sense, the face is the icon of the body, the place where the inner world of the person becomes manifest. The human face is the subtle yet visual autobiography of each person. Regardless of how concealed or hidden the inner story of your life is, you can never successfully hide from the world while you have a face. If we knew how to read the faces of others, we would be able to decipher the mysteries of their life stories. The face always reveals the soul; it is where the divinity of the inner life finds an echo and image. When you behold someone's face, you are gazing deeply into that person's life.

THE HOLINESS OF THE GAZE

In South America, a journalist friend of mine met an old Indian chief whom he would have loved to interview. The chief agreed, on the condition that they could have some time together beforehand. The journalist presumed that they would meet and just have a normal conversation. Instead, the chief took him aside and looked directly into his eyes in silence for a long time. Initially, this terrified my friend; he felt his life was totally exposed to the gaze and silence of this stranger. After a while, the journalist began to deepen his own gaze. Each continued this silent gazing for more than two hours. After this time, it seemed as if they had known each other all of their lives. There was no longer any need for the interview. In a certain sense, to gaze into the face of another is to gaze into the depth and entirety of his life.

We assume too readily that we share the one world with other people. It is true at the objective level that we inhabit the same physical space as other humans; the sky is, after all, the one visual constant that unites everyone's perception of being in the world. Yet this outer world offers no access to the inner world of an individual. At a deeper level, each person is the custodian of a completely private, individual world. Sometimes our beliefs, opinions, and thoughts are ultimately ways of consoling ourselves that we are not alone with the burden of a unique, inner world. It suits us to pretend that we all belong to the one world, but we are more alone than we realize. This aloneness is not simply the result of our being different from each other; it derives more from the fact that each of us is housed in a different body. The idea of human life being housed in a body is fascinating. For instance, when people come to visit your home, they come bodily. They bring all of their inner worlds, experiences, and memories into your house through the vehicle of their bodies. While they are visiting you, their lives are not elsewhere; they are totally there with you, before you, reaching out toward you. When the visit is over, their bodies stand up, walk out, and carry this hidden world away. This recognition also illuminates the mystery of making love. It is not just two bodies that are close, but rather two worlds; they circle each other and flow into each other. We are capable of such beauty, delight, and terror because of this infinite and unknown world within us.

THE INFINITY OF YOUR INTERIORITY

The human person is a threshold where many infinities meet. There is the infinity of space that reaches out into the depths of the cosmos and the infinity of time reaching back over billions of years. There is the infinity of the microcosm: one little speck on the top of your thumb contains a whole inner cosmos, but it is so tiny that it is not visible to the human eye. The infinity in the microscopic is as dazzling as that of the cosmos. However, the infinity that haunts everyone and which no one can finally quell is the infinity of one's own interiority. A world lies hidden behind each human face. In some faces the vulnerability of inner exposure to these depths becomes visible. When you look at some faces, you can see the turbulence of the infinite beginning to gather to the surface. This moment can open in a gaze from a stranger, or in a conversation with someone you know well. Suddenly, without their intending it or being conscious of it, their gaze becomes the vehicle of some primal inner presence. This gaze lasts for only a second. In that slightest interim, something more than the person looks out. Another infinity, as yet unborn, is dimly present. You feel that you are being looked at from the strangeness of the eternal. The infinity gazing out at you is from an ancient time. We cannot seal off the eternal. Unexpectedly and disturbingly, it gazes in at us through the sudden apertures in our patterned lives. A friend of mine who loves lace often says that it is the holes in the lace that render it beautiful. Our experience has this lace structure.

The human face carries mystery and is the exposure point of the mystery of the individual life. It is where the private, inner world of a person protrudes into the anonymous world. While the rest of the body is covered, the face is naked. The vulnerability of this nakedness issues a profound invitation for understanding and compassion. The human face is a meeting place of two unknowns: the infinity of the outer world and the unchartered, inner world to which each individual alone has access. This is the night world that lies behind the brightness of the visage. The smile on a face is a surprise or illumination. When the smile crosses the face, it is as if the inner night of this hidden world brightens suddenly. Heidegger said very beautifully that we are custodians of deep and ancient thresholds. In the human face you see that potential and the miracle of undying possibility.

The face is the pinnacle of the body. Your body is as ancient as the clay of the universe from which it is made; and your feet on the ground are a constant connection with the earth. Your feet bring your private clay in touch with the ancient, mother clay from which you first emerged.

Consequently, your face being at the top of your body signifies the ascent of your clay-life into intimacy and selfhood. It
is as if the clay of your body becomes intimate and personal
through the ever new expressions of your face. Beneath the
dome of the skull, the face is the place where your clay-life
takes on a real human presence.

THE FACE AND THE SECOND INNOCENCE

Your face is the icon of your life. In the human face, a life
looks out at the world and also looks in on itself. It is
frightening to behold a face in which bitterness and resentment have lodged. When a person's life has been bleak, much
of its negativity can remain unhealed. Since the negativity is
left untransfigured, the bleakness lodges in the face. The face,
instead of being a warm presence, has hardened to become a
mask. One of the oldest words for person is the Greek word
prosopon; and *prosopon* originally meant the mask that actors
wore in a Greek chorus. When bitterness, anger, or resentment are left untransfigured, the face becomes a mask. Yet
one also encounters the opposite, namely, the beautiful presence of an old face deeply lined and inscribed by time and
experience that has retained a lovely innocence. Even though
life may have moved wearily and painfully through such a
person, they have still managed not to let it corrode their
soul. In such a face a lovely luminosity shines out into the

world. It casts a tender light that radiates a sense of holiness and wholesomeness.

The face always reveals who you are, and what life has done to you. Yet it is difficult for you to see the shape of your own life; your life is too near you. Others can decipher much of your mystery from your face. Portrait artists admit that it is exceptionally difficult to render the human face. Traditionally, the eyes are said to be the windows of the soul. The mouth is also difficult to render in the individual portrait. In some strange way the line of the mouth seems to betray the contour of the life; a tight mouth often suggests meanness of spirit. There is a strange symmetry in the way the soul writes the story of its life in the contours of the face.

THE BODY IS THE ANGEL OF THE SOUL

The human body is beautiful. It is such a privilege to be embodied. You have a relationship to a place through the body. It is no wonder that humans have always been fascinated by place. Place offers us a home here; without place we would literally have no where. Landscape is the ultimate where; and in landscape the house that we call *home* is our intimate place. The home is decorated and personalized; it takes on the soul of the person who lives there and becomes the mirror of the spirit. Yet in the deepest sense, the body is the most intimate place. Your body is your clay home; your body is the only home that you have in this universe. It is in and through your body that your soul becomes visible and real for you. Your body is the home of your soul on earth.

Often there seems to be an uncanny appropriateness between the soul and the shape and physical presence of the body. This is not true in all instances, but frequently it yields an insight into the nature of a person's inner world. There is a secret relationship between our physical being and the rhythm of our soul. The body is the place where the soul shows itself. A friend from Connemara once said to me that the body is the angel of the soul. The body is the angel who expresses and minds the soul; we should always pay loving attention to our bodies. The body has often been a scapegoat for the deceptions and poisons of the mind. A primordial innocence surrounds the body, an incredible brightness and goodness. The body is the angel of the life.

The body can be home to a great range and intensity of presence. Theater is a striking illustration. An actor has enough internal space available to take in a character and let it inhabit him totally, so that the character's voice, mind, and action find subtle and immediate expression through the actor's body. The body of the actor becomes the character's presence. The most exuberant expression of the body is in dance. Dance theater is wonderful. The dance becomes fluent sculpture. The body shapes the emptiness poignantly and majestically. The exciting example of this in the Irish tradition is *sean nós* dancing, where the dancer mirrors in his body the wild flow of the traditional music.

The body is much sinned against, even in a religion based on the Incarnation. Religion has often presented the body as the source of evil, ambiguity, lust, and seduction. This is utterly false and irreverent. The body is sacred. The origin of much of this negative thinking is in a false interpretation of Greek philosophy. The Greeks were beautiful thinkers precisely because of the emphasis they placed on the divine. The divine haunted them, and they endeavored in language and concept to echo the divine and find some mirror for its presence. They were acutely aware of the gravity in the body and how it seemed to drag the divine too much toward the earth. They misconceived this attraction to the earth and saw in it a conflict with the world of the divine. They had no conception of the Incarnation, no inkling of the Resurrection.

When the Christian tradition incorporated Greek philosophy, it brought this dualism into its thought world. The soul was understood as beautiful, bright, and good. The desire to be with God belonged to the nature of the soul. Were it not for the unfortunate gravity of the body, the soul could constantly inhabit the eternal. In this way, a great suspicion of the body entered the Christian tradition. Coupled with this is the fact that a theology of sensual love never flowered in the Christian tradition. One of the few places the erotic appears is in the beautiful canticle the Song of Songs. It celebrates the sensuous and sensual with wonderful passion and gentleness. This text is an exception; and it is surprising that it was allowed into the Canon of Scripture. In subsequent Christian tradition, and especially among the Church Fathers, there was a deep suspicion of the body and a negative obsession with sexuality. Sex and sexuality were portrayed as a potential danger to one's eternal salvation. The Christian tradition has often undervalued and mistreated the sacred presence of the body. Artists, however, have been wonderfully inspired by the Christian tradition. A beautiful example is Bernini's *Teresa in Ecstasy*. Teresa's body is caught in the throes of an ecstacy where the sensuous and the mystical are no longer separable.

THE BODY AS MIRROR OF THE SOUL

The body is a sacrament. The old, traditional definition of sacrament captures this beautifully. A sacrament is a visible sign of invisible grace. In that definition there is a fine acknowledgment of how the unseen world comes to expression in the visible world. This desire for expression lies deep at the heart of the invisible world. All our inner life and intimacy of soul longs to find an outer mirror. It longs for a form in which it can be seen, felt, and touched. The body is the mirror where the secret world of the soul comes to expression. The body is a sacred threshold; and it deserves to be respected, minded, and understood in its spiritual nature.

This sense of the body is wonderfully expressed in an amazing phrase from the Catholic tradition: *The body is the temple of the Holy Spirit*. The Holy Spirit holds the intimacy and distance of the Trinity alert and personified. To describe the human body as the temple of the Holy Spirit recognizes that the body is suffused with wild and vital divinity. This theological insight shows that the sensuous is sacred in the deepest sense.

The body is also very truthful. You know from your own life that your body rarely lies. Your mind can deceive you and put all kinds of barriers between you and your nature; but your body does not lie. Your body tells you, if you attend to it, how your life is and whether you are living from your soul or from the labyrinths of your negativity. The body also has a wonderful intelligence. All of our movements, indeed everything we do, demands the most refined and detailed cooperation of each of our senses. The human body is the most complex, refined, and harmonious totality.

The body is your only home in the universe. It is your house of belonging here in the world. It is a very sacred temple. To spend time in silence before the mystery of your body brings you toward wisdom and holiness. It is unfortunate that often only when we are ill do we realize how tender, fragile, and precious is the house of belonging called the body. When you visit people who are ill or who are awaiting surgery, you can encourage them to have a conversation with the body area that is unwell. Suggest that they talk to it as a partner, thank it for all it has done, for what it has suffered, and ask forgiveness of it for whatever pressure it may have had to endure. Each part of the body holds the memory of its own experience.

Your body is, in essence, a crowd of different members who work in harmony to make your belonging in the world possible. We should avoid the false dualism that separates the soul from the body. The soul is not simply within the body, hidden somewhere within its recesses. The truth is rather the converse. Your body is in the soul, and the soul suffuses you completely. Therefore, all around you there is a secret and beautiful soul-light. This recognition suggests a new art of prayer: Close your eyes and relax into your body. Imagine a light all around you, the light of your soul. Then with your breath, draw that light into your body and bring it with your breath through every area of your body.

This is a lovely way to pray, because you are bringing the soul-light, the shadowed shelter that surrounds you, right into the physical earth and clay of your presence. One of the oldest meditations is to imagine the light coming into you, and then on your outward breath to imagine you are exhaling the darkness or an inner charcoal residue. People who are ill can be encouraged to pray physically in this way. When you bring cleansing, healing soul-light into your body, you heal the neglected, tormented places. Your body knows you very intimately; it is aware of your whole spirit and soul life. Far sooner than your mind, your body knows how privileged it is to be here. It is also aware of the presence of death. There is a wisdom in your physical, bodily presence that is luminous and profound. Frequently the illnesses that come to us result from our self-neglect and our failure to listen to the voice of the body. The inner voices of the body want to speak to us, to inform us of the truths beneath the fixed surface of our external lives.

FOR THE CELTS, THE VISIBLE AND THE INVISIBLE ARE ONE

The body has had such a low and negative profile in the world of spirituality because spirit has been understood more in terms of the air element than the earth element. The air is the region of the invisible; it is the region of breath and thought. When you confine spirit to this region alone, the physical becomes immediately diminished. This is a great mistake, for there is nothing in the universe as sensuous as God. The wildness of God is the sensuousness of God. Nature is the direct expression of the divine imagination. It is the most intimate reflection of God's sense of beauty. Nature is the mirror of the divine imagination and the mother of all sensuality; therefore it is unorthodox to understand spirit in terms of the invisible alone. Ironically, divinity and spirit derive their power and energy precisely from this tension between the visible and the invisible. Everything in the world of soul has a deep desire and longing for visible form; this is exactly where the power of the imagination lives.

The imagination is the faculty that bridges, co-presents, and co-articulates the visible and the invisible. In the Celtic world, for instance, there was a wonderful sense of how the visible and the invisible moved in and out of each other. In the West of Ireland, there are many stories about ghosts, spirits, or fairies who had a special association with particular places; to the mind of the local people these legends were as natural as the landscape. For instance, there is a tradition that a lone bush in a field should never be cut down. The implication is that it may be a secret gathering place for spirits. There are many other places that are considered to be fairy forts. The local people would never build there or intrude in any way on that sacred ground.

THE CHILDREN OF LIR

One of the amazing aspects of the Celtic world is the idea of shape shifting. This becomes possible only when the physical is animate and passionate. The essence or soul of a thing is not limited to its particular or present shape. Soul has a fluency and energy that is not to be caged within any fixed form. Consequently, in the Celtic tradition there is a fascinating interflow between soul and matter and between time and eternity. This rhythm also includes and engages the human body.

The human body is a mirror and expression of the world of soul. One of the most poignant illustrations of this in the Celtic tradition is the beautiful legend of the children of Lir.

Central to the ancient Irish mind was the mythological world of the Tuatha Dé Dannan, the tribe that lived under the surface of the earth in Ireland; this myth has imbued the whole landscape with a numinous depth and presence. Lir was a chieftain in the world of the Tuatha Dé Dannan, and he had conflict with the king in that region. In order to resolve the conflict, a marriage agreement was made. The king had three daughters, and he offered Lir one of them in marriage. They married and had two children. Shortly thereafter they had two more children, but then unfortunately Lir's wife died. Lir came again to the king, and the king gave him his second daughter. She watched over him and the children, but she became jealous when she saw that he dedicated most of his attention to the children. She noticed that even her own father, the king, had a very special affection for the children. Over the years, the jealousy grew in her heart until she finally took the children in her chariot and, with a touch of her druidic magic wand, turned them into four swans. They were condemned to spend nine hundred years in exile on the oceans around Ireland. Even though they were in swan form, they still retained their human minds and full human identities. When Christianity came to Ireland, they were finally returned to human form, but as old decrepit people. There is such poignance in the description of their journey in the wilderness as animal shapes imbued with human presence. This is a deeply Celtic story that shows how the world of nature finds a bridge to the animal world. The story also demonstrates that there is a profound confluence of intimacy between the human and the animal world. When they were swans, the song of the children of Lir had the power to heal and console people. The pathos of the story is deepened by the vulnerable openness of the animal world to the human.

The animals are more ancient than us. They were here for millennia before humans surfaced on the earth. Animals are our ancient brothers and sisters. They enjoy a seamless presence—a lyrical unity with the earth. Animals live outside in the wind, in the waters, in the mountains, and in the clay. The knowing of the earth is in them. The Zen-like silence and thereness of the landscape is mirrored in the silence and solitude of animals. Animals know nothing of Freud, Jesus, Buddha, Wall Street, the Pentagon, or the Vatican. They live outside the politics of human intention. Somehow they already inhabit the eternal. The Celtic mind recognized the ancient belonging and knowing of the animal world. The dignity, beauty, and wisdom of the animal world was not diminished by any false hierarchy or human arrogance. Somewhere in the Celtic mind was a grounding perception that humans are the inheritors of this deeper world. This finds playful expression in the following ninth-century poem.

THE SCHOLAR AND HIS CAT

I and Pangur Bán my cat,
'Tis like a task we are at:
Hunting mice is his delight,
Hunting words I sit all night

Better far than praise of men
'Tis to sit with book and pen;
Pangur bears me no ill will
He too plies his simple skill.

'Tis a merry thing to see
At our tasks how glad are we,
When at home we sit and find
Entertainment to our mind.

Oftentimes a mouse will stray
In the hero Pangur's way;
Oftentimes my keen thought set
Takes a meaning in its net.

'Gainst the wall he sets his eye
Full and fierce and sharp and sly;
'Gainst the wall of knowledge I
All my little wisdom try.

When a mouse darts from its den
O how glad is Pangur then!
O what gladness do I prove
When I solve the doubts I love!

So in peace our tasks we ply,
Pangur Bán, my cat and I;
In our arts we find our bliss,
I have mine and he has his.

Practice every day has made
Pangur perfect in his trade;
I get wisdom day and night
Turning darkness into light.

(TRANS. ROBIN FLOWER)

For the Celts, the world is always latently and actively spiritual. The depth of this interflow is also apparent in the power of language in the Celtic world. Language itself had power to cause events and to divine events yet to happen. Chants and spells could actually reverse a whole course of negative destiny and bring forth something new and good. In the Celtic world, and especially in the Celtic world of the senses, there was no barrier between soul and body. Each was natural to the other. The soul was the sister of the body, the body the sister of the soul. As yet there was no negative splitting of dualistic Christian morality, which later did so much damage to these two lovely and enfolded presences. The world of Celtic consciousness enjoyed this unified and lyrical sensuous spirituality.

Light is the mother of life. The sun brings light or color. It causes grasses, crops, leaves, and flowers to grow. The sun brings forth the erotic charge of the curved earth; it awakens her wild sensuousness. In this Gaelic poem, the sun is worshiped as the eye and face of God. The rich vitalism of the Celtic sensibility finds lyrical expression here.

> The eye of the great God,
> The eye of the god of glory,
> The eye of the king of hosts,
> The eye of the king of the living.

> Pouring upon us
>   At each time and season,
> Pouring upon us
>   gently and generously

> Glory to thee
>   Thou glorious sun.
> Glory to thee, thou son
>   Face of the God of life.

> (TRANS. A. CARMICHAEL)

A Spirituality of Transfiguration

Spirituality is the art of transfiguration. We should not force ourselves to change by hammering our lives into any predetermined shape. We do not need to operate according to the idea of a predetermined program or plan for our lives. Rather, we need to practice a new art of attention to the inner rhythm of our days and lives. This attention brings a new awareness of our own human and divine presence. A dramatic example of this kind of transfiguration is one all parents know. You watch your children carefully, but one day they surprise you: You still recognize them, but your knowledge of them is insufficient. You have to start listening to them all over again.

It is far more creative to work with the idea of mindfulness rather than with the idea of will. Too often people try to change their lives by using the will as a kind of hammer to beat their life into proper shape. The intellect identifies the goal of the program, and the will accordingly forces the life into that shape. This way of approaching the sacredness of one's own presence is externalist and violent. It brings you falsely outside yourself, and you can spend years lost in the wildernesses of your own mechanical, spiritual programs. You can perish in a famine of your own making.

If you work with a different rhythm, you will come easily and naturally home to yourself. Your soul knows the geography of your destiny. Your soul alone has the map of your future, therefore you can trust this indirect, oblique side of yourself. If you do, it will take you where you need to go, but more important it will teach you a kindness of rhythm in your journey. There are no general principles for this art of being. Yet the signature of this unique journey is inscribed deeply in each soul. If you attend to yourself and seek to come into your presence, you will find exactly the right rhythm for your own life. The senses are generous pathways that can bring you home.

A renewal, indeed a complete transfiguration of your life, can come through attention to your senses. Your senses are the guides to take you deep into the inner world of your heart. The greatest philosophers admit that to a large degree all knowledge comes through the senses. The senses are our bridges to the world. Human skin is porous; the world flows through you. Your senses are large pores that let the world in. By being attuned to the wisdom of your senses, you will never become an exile in your own life, an outsider lost in an external spiritual place that your will and intellect have constructed.

THE SENSES AS THRESHOLDS OF SOUL

For too long, we have believed that the divine is outside us. This belief has strained our longing disastrously. This makes us lonely, since it is human longing that makes us holy. The most beautiful thing about us is our longing; this longing is spiritual and has great depth and wisdom. If you focus your longing on a faraway divinity, you put an unfair strain on your longing. Thus it often happens that the longing reaches out toward the distant divine, but because it overstrains itself, it bends back to become cynicism, emptiness, or negativity. This can destroy your sensibility. Yet we do not need to put any strain whatever on our longing. If we believe that the body is in the soul and the soul is divine ground, then the presence of the divine is completely here, close with us.

Being in the soul, the body makes the senses thresholds of soul. When your senses open out to the world, the first presence they encounter is the presence of your soul. To be sensual or sensuous is to be in the presence of your own soul. Wordsworth, careful of the dignity of the senses, wrote that "pleasure is the tribute we owe to our dignity as human beings." This is a profoundly spiritual perspective. Your senses link you intimately with the divine within you and around you. Attunement to the senses can limber up the stiffened belief and gentle the hardened outlook. It can warm and heal the atrophied feelings that are the barriers exiling us from ourselves and separating us from each other. Then we are no longer in exile from the wonderful harvest of divinity that is always secretly gathering within us. Though we will consider each of the senses specifically, it is important to acknowledge that the senses always work compositely. The senses overlap. We can see this in the different responses people have to color, which indicates that colors are not perceived merely visually.

THE EYE IS LIKE THE DAWN

The first sense we will consider is the sense of sight or vision. The human eye is one place where the intensity of human presence becomes uniquely focused and available. The universe finds its deepest reflection and belonging in the human eye. I imagine the mountains dreaming of the coming of vision. The eye, when it opens, is like the dawn breaking in the night. When it opens, a new world is there. The eye is also the mother of distance. When the eye opens, it shows that others and the world are outside us, distant from us. The spur of tension that has enlivened all of Western philosophy is the desire to bring subject and object together. Perhaps it is the eye as mother of distance that splits the subject from the object. Yet infinity somehow invests our perception of every object. Joseph Brodsky said beautifully, An object makes infinity private.

Yet in a wonderful way, the eye as mother of distance makes us wonder at the mystery and otherness of everything outside us. In this sense, the eye is also the mother of intimacy, bringing everything close to us. When you really gaze at something, you bring it inside you. One could write a beautiful spirituality on the holiness of the gaze. The opposite of the gaze is the intrusive stare. When you are stared at, the eye of the Other becomes tyrannical. You have become the object of the Other's stare in a humiliating, invasive, and threatening way.

When you really look deeply at something, it becomes part of you. This is one of the sinister aspects of television. People are constantly looking at empty and false images; these impoverished images are filling up the inner world of the heart. The modern world of image and electronic media is reminiscent of Plato's wonderful allegory of the cave. The prisoners are in one line, chained together, looking at the wall of the cave. The fire behind them casts images onto the wall. The prisoners believe that what they see on the wall of that cave is reality. Yet all they are seeing are shadows of reflections. Television and the computer world are great empty shadowlands. To look at something that can gaze back at you, or that has a reserve and depth, can heal your eyes and deepen your sense of vision.

There are those who are physically blind; they have lived all their lives in a monoscape of darkness. They have never seen a wave, a stone, a star, a flower, the sky, or the face of another human being. Yet there are others with perfect vision who are absolutely blind. The Irish painter Tony O'Malley is a wonderful artist of the invisible; in a lovely introduction to his work, the English artist Patrick Heron said, "In contrast to most people, Tony O'Malley walks around with his eyes open."

Many of us have made our world so familiar that we do not see it anymore. An interesting question to ask yourself at night is, What did I really see this day? You could be surprised at what you did not see. Maybe your eyes were unconditioned reflexes operating all day without any real mindfulness or recognition; while you looked out from yourself, you never gazed or really attended to anything. The field of vision is always complex, and when your eyes look out, they cannot see everything. If you try to have a full field of vision, then details become unspecified and blurred; if you focus on one aspect of it, then you really see that, but you miss out on the larger picture. The human eye is always selecting what it wants to see and also evading what it does not want to see. The crucial question then is, What criteria do we use to decide what we like to see and to avoid seeing what we do not want to see? Many limited and negative lives issue directly from this narrowness of vision.

It is a startling truth that how you see and what you see determine how and who you will be. An interesting way of beginning to do some interior work is to explore your particular style of seeing. Ask yourself, What way do I behold the world? Through this question you will discover your specific pattern of seeing.

STYLES OF VISION

To the fearful eye, all is threatening. When you look toward the world in a fearful way, all you see and concentrate on are things that can damage and threaten you. The fearful eye is always besieged by threat.

To the greedy eye, everything can be possessed. Greed is one of the powerful forces in the modern Western world. It is sad that a greedy person can never enjoy what they have, because they are always haunted by that which they do not yet possess. This can refer to land, books, companies, ideas, money, or art. The motor and agenda of greed is always the same. Joy is possession, but sadly possession is ever restless; it has an inner insatiable hunger. Greed is poignant because it is always haunted and emptied by future possibility; it can never engage presence. However, the more sinister aspect of greed is its ability to sedate and extinguish desire. It destroys the natural innocence of desire, dismantles its horizons, and replaces them with a driven and atrophied possessiveness. This greed is now poisoning the earth and impoverishing its people. Having has become the sinister enemy of being.

To the judgmental eye, everything is closed in definitive frames. When the judgmental eye looks out, it sees things in terms of lines and squares. It is always excluding and separating, and therefore it never sees in a compassionate or celebratory way. To see is to judge. Sadly, the judgmental eye is always equally harsh with itself. It sees only the images of its tormented interiority projected outward from itself. The judgmental eye harvests the reflected surface and calls it truth. It enjoys neither the forgiveness nor imagination to see deeper into the ground of things where truth is paradox. An externalist, image-driven culture is the corollary of such an ideology of facile judgment.

To the resentful eye, everything is begrudged. People who have allowed the canker of resentment into their vision can never enjoy who they are or what they have. They are always looking out toward others with resentment. Perhaps they are resentful because they see others as more beautiful, more gifted, or richer than themselves. The resentful eye lives out of its poverty and forgets its own inner harvest.

To the indifferent eye, nothing calls or awakens. Indifference is one of the hallmarks of our times. It is said that indifference is necessary for power; to hold control one has to be successfully indifferent to the needs and vulnerabilities of those under control. Thus indifference calls for a great commitment to nonvision. To ignore things demands incredible mental energy. Without even knowing it, indifference can place you beyond the frontiers of compassion, healing, and love. When you become indifferent, you give all your power away. Your imagination becomes fixated in the limbo of cynicism and despair.

To the inferior eye, everyone else is greater. Others are more beautiful, brilliant, and gifted than you. The inferior eye is always looking away from its own treasures. It can never celebrate its own presence and potential. The inferior eye is blind to its secret beauty. The human eye was never designed to look up in a way that inflates the Other to superiority, nor to look down, reducing the Other to inferiority. To look someone in the eye is a nice testament to truth, courage, and expectation. Each one stands on common, but different, ground.

To the loving eye, everything is real. This art of love is neither sentimental nor naive. Such love is the greatest criterion of truth, celebration, and reality. Kathleen Raine, a Scottish poet, says that unless you see a thing in the light of love, you do not see it at all. Love is the light in which we see light. Love is the light in which we see each thing in its true origin, nature, and destiny. If we could look at the world in a loving way, then the world would rise up before us full of invitation, possibility, and depth.

The loving eye can even coax pain, hurt, and violence toward transfiguration and renewal. The loving eye is bright because it is autonomous and free. It can look lovingly upon anything. The loving vision does not become entangled in the agenda of power, seduction, opposition, or complicity. Such vision is creative and subversive. It rises above the pathetic arithmetic of blame and judgment and engages experience at the level of its origin, structure, and destiny. The loving eye sees through and beyond image and effects the deepest change. Vision is central to your presence and creativity. To recognize *how* you see things can bring you self-knowledge and enable you to glimpse the wonderful treasures your life secretly holds.

TASTE AND SPEECH

The sense of taste is subtle and complex. The tongue is the organ of taste and also the organ of speech. Taste is one of the casualties in our modern world. Since we are under such pressure and stress, we have so little time to taste the food we eat. An old friend of mine often says that food is love. At a meal in her house one has to take one's time and bring patience and mindfulness to the meal.

We have no longer any sense of the decorum appropriate to eating. We have lost the sense of ritual, presence, and intimacy that were elemental to any meal; we no longer sit down to meals in the old way. One of the most famous qualities of the Celtic people was hospitality. A stranger always received a meal. This courtesy was observed before any other business was undertaken. When you celebrate a meal, you also taste flavors of which you are normally unaware. Much modern food lacks flavor completely; even while it is growing, it is forced with artificial fertilizers and sprayed with chemicals. Consequently it has none of the taste of nature. As a result, for most people, their sense of taste has become severely dulled. The fast-food metaphor provides a deep clue to the poverty of sensibility and lack of taste in modern culture. This is also clearly mirrored in our use of language. The tongue, the organ of taste, is also the organ of speech. Many of the words we use are of the fast-food spiritual variety. These words are too thin to echo experience; they are too weak to bring the inner mystery of things to real expression. In our rapid and externalized world, language has become ghostlike, abbreviated to code and label. Words that would mirror the soul carry the loam of substance and the shadow of the divine.

The sense of silence and darkness behind the words in more ancient cultures, particularly in folk culture, is absent in the modern use of language. Language is full of acronyms; nowadays we are impatient of words that carry with them histories and associations. Rural people, and particularly people in the West of Ireland, have a great sense of language. There is a sense of phrasing that is poetic and alert. The force of the intuition and the spark of recognition slip swiftly into deft phrase. One of the factors that makes spoken English in Ireland so interesting is the colorful ghost of the Gaelic language behind it. This imbues the use of English with great color, nuance, and power. Yet the attempt to destroy Gaelic was one of the most destructive acts of violence of the colonization of Ireland by England. Gaelic is such a poetic and powerful language, it carries the Irish memory. When you steal a people's language, you leave their soul bewildered.

Poetry is the place where language in its silence is most beautifully articulated. Poetry is the language of silence.

If you look at a page of prose, it is crowded with words. If you look at a page of poetry, the slim word shapes are couched in the empty whiteness of the page. The page is a place of silence where the contour of the word is edged and the expression is heightened in an intimate way. It is interesting to look at your language and the words that you tend to use to see if you can hear a stillness or silence. One way to invigorate and renew your language is to expose yourself to poetry. In poetry your language will find cleansing illumination and sensuous renewal.

FRAGRANCE AND BREATH

The sense of smell or fragrance is deft and immediate. Experts tell us that smell is the most faithful of all the senses in terms of memory. The smells of one's childhood still remain within. It is incredible how a simple scent on a street or in a room can bring you back years to an experience you had long forgotten. Animals, of course, work wonderfully with the sense of smell. To take dogs for a walk is to realize how differently they experience landscape. They are glued to trails of scent and enjoy a complete adventure, tracing invisible smell pathways everywhere. Each day we breathe 23,040 times; we have 5 million olfactory cells. A sheepdog has 220 million such cells. The sense of smell is so powerful in the animal world because it assists survival by alerting the animal to danger. The sense of smell is vital to the sense of life.

Traditionally, the breath was understood as the pathway through which the soul entered the body. Breaths come in

pairs except the first breath and the last breath. At the deepest level, breath is sister of spirit. One of the most ancient
words for spirit is the Hebrew word *Ruah*; this is also the
word for air or wind. Ruah also denotes pathos, passion, and
emotion—a state of the soul. The word suggests that God
was like breath and wind because of the incredible passion
and pathos of divinity. In the Christian tradition, the understanding of the mystery of the Trinity also suggests that the
Holy Spirit arises within the Trinity through the breathing of
the Father and the Son; the technical term is *spiratio*. This
ancient recognition links the wild creativity of the Spirit with
the breath of the soul in the human person. Breath is also
deeply appropriate as a metaphor because divinity, like
breath, is invisible. The world of thought resides in the air.
All of our thoughts happen in the air element. Our greatest
thoughts come to us from the generosity of the air. It is here
that the idea of inspiration is rooted—you inspire or breathe
in the thoughts concealed in the air element. Inspiration can
never be programmed. You can prepare, making yourself
ready to be inspired, yet it is spontaneous and unpredictable.
It breaks the patterns of repetition and expectation.
Inspiration is always a surprising visitor.

To labor in the world of learning, research, or in the artistic world, one attempts again and again to refine one's sense
of readiness so that the great images or thoughts can approach
and be received. The sense of smell includes the sensuality of

fragrance, but the dynamic of breathing also takes in the deep world of prayer and meditation, where through the rhythm of the breath you come down into your own primordial level of soul. Through breath meditation, you begin to experience a place within you that is absolutely intimate with the divine ground. Your breathing and the rhythm of your breathing can return you to your ancient belonging, to the house, as Eckhart says, that you have never left, where you always live: the house of spiritual belonging.

True Listening Is Worship

With the sense of hearing, we listen to creation. One of the great thresholds in reality is the threshold between sound and silence. All good sounds have silence near, behind, and within them. The first sound that every human hears is the sound of the mother's heartbeat in the dark lake water of the womb. This is the reason for our ancient resonance with the drum as a musical instrument. The sound of the drum brings us consolation because it brings us back to that time when we were at one with the mother's heartbeat. That was a time of complete belonging. No separation had yet opened; we were completely in unity with another person. P. J. Curtis, the great Irish authority on rhythm and blues music, often says that the search for meaning is really the search for the lost chord. When the lost chord is discovered by humankind, the discord in the world will be healed and the symphony of the universe will come into complete harmony with itself.

It is lovely to have the gift of hearing. It is said that deafness is worse than blindness because you are isolated in an inner world of terrible silence. Even though you can see people and the world around you, to be outside the reach of sound and the human voice is very lonely. There is a very important distinction to be made between listening and hearing. Sometimes we listen to things, but we never hear them. True listening brings us in touch even with that which is unsaid and unsayable. Sometimes the most important thresholds of mystery are places of silence. To be genuinely spiritual is to have great respect for the possibilities and presence of silence. Martin Heidegger says that true listening is worship. When you listen with your soul, you come into rhythm and unity with the music of the universe. Through friendship and love, you learn to attune yourself to the silence, to the thresholds of mystery where your life enters the life of your beloved and the beloved's life enters yours.

Poets are people who become utterly dedicated to the threshold where silence and language meet. One of the crucial tasks of the poet's vocation is to find his or her own voice. When you begin to write, you feel you are writing fine poetry; then you read other poets only to find that they have already written similar poems. You realize that you were unconsciously imitating them. It takes a long time to sift through

the more superficial voices of your own gift in order to enter
into the deep signature and tonality of your Otherness. When
you speak from that deep, inner voice, you are really speaking
from the unique tabernacle of your own presence. There is a
voice within you that no one, not even you, has ever heard.
Give yourself the opportunity of silence and begin to develop
your listening in order to hear, deep within yourself, the
music of your own spirit.

Music is after all the most perfect sound to meet the
silence. When you really listen to music, you begin to hear
the beautiful way it constellates and textures the silence, how
it brings out the hidden mystery of silence. The echo of the
gentle membrane where sound meets silence becomes deftly
audible. Long before humans arrived on earth, there was an
ancient music here. Yet one of the most beautiful gifts that
humans have brought to the earth is music. In great music,
the ancient longing of the earth finds a voice. The wonderful
conductor Sergiu Celibidache said, "We do not create music;
we only create the conditions so that she can appear." Music
ministers to the silence and solitude of nature; it is one of the
most powerful, immediate, and intimate of sensuous experiences. Music is, perhaps, the art form that brings us closest to
the eternal because it changes immediately and irreversibly
the way we experience time. When we are listening to beautiful music, we enter into the eternal dimension of time.
Transitory, broken linear time fades away, and we come into

the circle of belonging within the eternal. The Irish writer Sean O'Faolain said, "In the presence of great music we have no alternative but to live nobly."

THE LANGUAGE OF TOUCH

Our sense of touch connects us to the world in an intimate way. As the mother of distance, the eye shows us that we are outside things. There is a magnificent piece of sculpture by Rodin called *The Embrace*. The sculpture shows two bodies reaching for each other, straining toward the kiss. All distance is broken in the magic of this kiss; two distanced ones have finally reached each other. Touch and the world of touch bring us out of the anonymity of distance into the intimacy of belonging. Humans use their hands to touch—to explore, to trace, and to feel the world outside of them. Hands are beautiful. Kant said that the hand is the visible expression of the mind. With your hands, you reach out to touch the world. In human touch, hands find the hands, face, or body of the Other. Touch brings presence home. The activity of touch brings us close to the world of the Other. It is the opposite of the eye, which readily translates its objects into intellectual terms. The eye appropriates according to its own logic. But touch confirms the Otherness of the body it touches. It cannot appropriate, it can only bring its objects closer and closer. We use the word *touching* to describe a story that moves us deeply. Touch is the sense through which we experience pain. There is nothing hesitant or blurred in the contact that pain makes with us. It reaches the core of our identity directly, awakening our fragility and desperation.

It is recognized now that every child needs to be touched. Touch communicates belonging, tenderness, and warmth, which fosters self-confidence, self-worth, and poise in the child. Touch has such power because we live inside the wonderful world of skin. Our skin is alive and breathing, always active and ever present. Human beings share such tenderness and fragility because we live not within shells but within skin, which is always sensitive to the force, touch, and presence of the world.

Touch is one of the most immediate and direct of the senses. The language of touch is a language in itself. Touch is also subtle and distinctive and holds within itself great refinement of memory. A concert pianist came to visit a friend. He asked her if she would like him to play something for her. He said, "At the moment I have a lovely piece from Schubert in my hands."

The world of touch includes the whole world of sexuality; this is probably the most tender aspect of human presence. When you are sexual with someone, you have let them right into your world. The world of sexuality is a sacred world of presence. The world of Eros is one of the devastated casualties of contemporary commercialism and greed. George Steiner has written powerfully about this. He shows how the words of intimacy, the night words of eros and affection, the secret words of love, have been vacated in the neon day of greed and consumerism. We desperately need to retrieve these gentle and sacred words of touch in order to be able to engage our full human nature. When you look at your inner world of soul, ask yourself how your sense of touch has developed. How do you actually touch things? Are you alive or awakened to the power of touch both as a sensuous and tender and healing force? A retrieval of touch can bring a new depth into your life; and it can heal, strengthen you, and bring you closer to yourself.

Touch is such an immediate sense. It can bring you in from the false world, the famine world of exile and image. Rediscovering the sense of touch returns you to the hearth of your own spirit, enabling you to experience again warmth, tenderness, and belonging. At the highest moments of human intensity, words become silent. Then the language of touch really speaks. When you are lost in the black valley of pain, words grow frail and dumb. To be embraced and held warmly brings the only shelter and consolation. Conversely, when you are completely happy, touch becomes an ecstatic language.

Touch offers the deepest clue to the mystery of encounter, awakening, and belonging. It is the secret, affective content of every connection and association. The energy, warmth, and invitation of touch come ultimately from the divine. The

Holy Spirit is the wild and passionate side of God, the tactile spirit whose touch is around you, bringing you close to yourself and to others. The Holy Spirit makes these distances attractive and laces them with fragrances of affinity and belonging. Graced distances make strangers friends. Your beloved and your friends were once strangers. Somehow at a particular time, they came from the distance toward your life. Their arrival seemed so accidental and contingent. Now your life is unimaginable without them. Similarly, your identity and vision are composed of a certain constellation of ideas and feelings that surfaced from the depths of distance within you. To lose these now would be to lose yourself. You live and move on divine ground. This is what St. Augustine said of God: "You are more intimate to me than I am to myself." The subtle immediacy of God, the Holy Spirit, touches your soul and tenderly weaves your ways and your days.

CELTIC SENSUOUSNESS

The world of Celtic spirituality is completely at home with the rhythm and wisdom of the senses. When you read Celtic nature poetry, you see that all the senses are alerted: You hear the sound of the winds, you taste the fruits, and above all you get a wonderful sense of how nature touches human presence. Celtic spirituality also has a great awareness of the sense of vision, particularly in relation to the spirit world. The Celtic eye has a great sense of that interim world between the invisible and the visible. This is referred to in scholarship as the *imaginal world*, the world where the angels live. The Celtic eye loves this interim world. In Celtic spirituality, we find a new bridge between the visible and the invisible; this comes to expression beautifully in its poetry and blessings. These two worlds are no longer separate. They flow naturally, gracefully, and lyrically in and out of each other.

A Blessing for the Senses

May your body be blessed.
May you realize that your body is a faithful and beautiful
friend of your soul.
And may you be peaceful and joyful and recognize that your
senses are sacred thresholds.
May you realize that holiness is mindful, gazing, feeling,
hearing, and touching.
May your senses gather you and bring you home.
May your senses always enable you to celebrate the universe
and the mystery and possibilities in your presence here.
May the Eros of the Earth bless you.

THREE

SOLITUDE IS LUMINOUS

THE WORLD OF THE SOUL IS SECRET

I was born in a limestone valley. To live in a valley is to enjoy a private sky. All around, life is framed by the horizon. The horizon shelters life yet constantly calls the eye to new frontiers and possibilities. The mystery of this landscape is further intensified by the presence of the ocean. For millions of years, an ancient conversation has continued between the chorus of the ocean and the silence of the stone.

No two stone shapes in this landscape are the same. Each stone has a different face. Often the angle of the light falls gently enough to bring out the shy presence of each stone. Here, it feels as if a wild, surrealistic God laid down the whole landscape. These stones, ever patient, ever still, continue to praise the silence of time. The Irish landscape is full of memory; it holds the ruins and traces of ancient civilization. There is a curvature in the landscape, a color and shape that constantly frustrate the eye anxious for symmetry or linear simplicity. The poet W. B. Yeats, in referring to this landscape, speaks of "that stern colour and that delicate line that are our secret discipline." Every few miles of road the landscape changes; it always surprises, offering ever new vistas that surprise the eye and call the imagination. This landscape has a wild yet serene complexity. In a sense, this reflects the nature of Celtic consciousness.

The Celtic mind was never drawn to the single line; it avoided ways of seeing and being that seek satisfaction in certainty. The Celtic mind had a wonderful respect for the mystery of the circle and the spiral. The circle is one of the oldest and most powerful symbols. The world is a circle; the sun and moon are too. Even time itself has a circular nature; the day and the year build to a circle. At its most intimate level so is the life of each individual. The circle never gives itself completely to the eye or to the mind but offers a trusting hospitality to that which is complex and mysterious; it embraces depth and height together. The circle never reduces the mystery to a single direction or preference. Patience with this reserve is one of the profound recognitions of the Celtic mind. The world of the soul is secret. The secret and the sacred are sisters. When the secret is not respected, the sacred vanishes.

Consequently, reflection should not shine too severe or aggressive a light in on the world of the soul. The light in Celtic consciousness is a penumbral light.

THE DANGER OF NEON VISION

There is an unprecedented spiritual hunger in our times. More and more people are awakening to the inner world. A thirst and hunger for the eternal is coming alive in their souls; this is a new form of consciousness. Yet one of the damaging aspects of this spiritual hunger is the way it sees everything in such a severe and insistent light. The light of modern consciousness is not gentle or reverent; it lacks graciousness in the presence of mystery; it wants to unriddle and control the unknown. Modern consciousness is similar to the harsh and brilliant white light of a hospital operating theater. This neon light is too direct and clear to befriend the shadowed world of the soul. It is not hospitable to what is reserved and hidden. The Celtic mind had a wonderful respect for the mystery and depth of the individual soul.

The Celts recognized that the shape of each soul is different; the spiritual clothing one person wears can never fit the soul of another. It is interesting that the word *revelation* comes from *re-valere*, literally, "to veil again." The world of the soul is glimpsed through the opening in a veil that closes again. There is no direct, permanent, or public access to the divine.

Each destiny has a unique curvature and must find its own spiritual belonging and direction. Individuality is the only gateway to spiritual potential and blessing.

When the spiritual search is too intense and hungry, the soul stays hidden. The soul was never meant to be seen completely. It is more at home in a light that is hospitable to shadow. Before electricity, people used candlelight at night. The ideal light to befriend the darkness, it gently opens up caverns in the darkness and prompts the imagination into activity. The candle allows the darkness to keep its secrets. There is shadow and color within every candle flame. Candlelight perception is the most respectful and appropriate form of light with which to approach the inner world. It does not force our tormented transparency upon the mystery. The glimpse is sufficient. Candlelight perception has the finesse and reverence appropriate to the mystery and autonomy of soul. Such perception is at home at the threshold. It neither needs nor desires to invade the *temenos* where the divine lives.

In our times, the language of psychology is used to approach the soul. Psychology is a wonderful science. In many ways, it has been the explorer whose heroic adventure discovered the uncharted inner world. In our culture of sensate immediacy, much psychology has abandoned the fecundity and reverence of myth and stands under the strain of neon consciousness, powerless to retrieve or open the depth and density of the world of soul. Celtic mysticism recognizes that rather than trying to expose the soul or offer it our fragile care, we should let the soul find us and care for us. Celtic mysticism is tender to the senses and devoid of spiritual aggression. The stories, poetry, and prayer of the Celts find expression in a language that is obviously prediscursive. It is a language of lyrical and reverential observation. Often it is reminiscent of the purity of the Japanese haiku. It bypasses the knottedness of narcissistic, self-reflexive language to create a lucid shape of words through which the numinous depths of nature and divinity can glisten. Celtic spirituality recognizes wisdom and the slow light, which can guard and deepen your life. When your soul awakens, your destiny becomes urgent with creativity.

Though destiny reveals itself slowly and partially, we sense its intention in the human countenance. I have always been fascinated by human presence in a landscape. When you walk the mountains and meet another person, you become acutely aware of the human face as an icon cast against the wilderness of nature. The face is a threshold where a world looks out and a world looks in on itself. The face brings these two worlds together. Behind each human face is a hidden world that no one can see. The beauty of the spiritual is its depth of inner friendship, which can totally change everything you touch, see, and feel. In a sense, the face is where the individual soul becomes obliquely visible. Yet the soul remains fugitive because the face cannot express directly everything we intuit and feel. Nevertheless, with age and memory the face gradually mirrors the journey of the soul. The older the face, the richer its mirroring.

TO BE BORN IS TO BE CHOSEN

To be born is to be chosen. No one is here by accident. Each one of us was sent here for a special destiny. When a fact is read in a spiritual way, its deeper meaning often emerges. When you consider the moment of conception, there are endless possibilities. Yet in most cases, only one child is conceived. This seems to suggest that a certain selectivity is already at work. This selectivity intimates a sheltering providence that dreamed you, created you, and always minds you. You were not consulted on the major factors that shaped your destiny: when you were to be born; where you would be born; to whom you would be born. Imagine the difference it would have made to your life had you been born into the house next door. Your identity was not offered for your choosing. In other words, a special destiny was prepared for you. But you were also given freedom and creativity to go beyond the given, to make a new set of relationships and to forge an ever new identity, inclusive of the old but not limited to it. This is the secret pulse of growth, which is quietly at work behind the outer facade of your life. Destiny sets the outer frame of experience and life; freedom finds and fills its inner form.

For millions of years, before you arrived here, the dream of your individuality was carefully prepared. You were sent to a shape of destiny in which you would be able to express the special gift you bring to the world. Sometimes this gift may involve suffering and pain that can neither be accounted for nor explained. There is a unique destiny for each person. Each one of us has something to do here that can be done by no one else. If someone else could fulfill your destiny, then they would be in your place, and you would not be here. It is in the depths of your life that you will discover the invisible necessity that has brought you here. When you begin to decipher this, your gift and giftedness come alive. Your heart quickens and the urgency of living rekindles your creativity.

If you can awaken this sense of destiny, you come into rhythm with your life. You fall out of rhythm when you renege on your potential and talent, when you settle for the mediocre as a refuge from the call. When you lose rhythm, your life becomes wearyingly deliberate or anonymously automatic. Rhythm is the secret key to balance and belonging. This will not collapse into false contentment or passivity. It is the rhythm of a dynamic equilibrium, a readiness of spirit, a poise that is not self-centered. This sense of rhythm is ancient. All life came out of the ocean; each one of us comes out of the waters of the womb; the ebb and flow of the tides is alive in the ebb and flow of our breathing. When you are in rhythm with your nature, nothing destructive can touch you.

Providence is at one with you; it minds you and brings you to your new horizons. To be spiritual is to be in rhythm.

THE CELTIC UNDERWORLD AS RESONANCE

I often think that the inner world is like a landscape. Here, in our limestone landscape, there are endless surprises. It is lovely to be on top of a mountain and to discover a spring well gushing forth from beneath the heavy rocks. Such a well has a long biography of darkness and silence. It comes from the heart of the mountain, where no human eye has ever gazed. The surprise of the well suggests the archaic resources of consciousness awakening within us. With a sudden freshness, new springs come alive within.

The silence of landscape conceals vast presence. Place is not simply location. A place is a profound individuality. Its surface texture of grass and stone is blessed by rain, wind, and light. With complete attention, landscape celebrates the liturgy of the seasons, giving itself unreservedly to the passion of the goddess. The shape of a landscape is an ancient and silent form of consciousness. Mountains are huge contemplatives. Rivers and streams offer voice; they are the tears of the earth's joy and despair. The earth is full of soul. Plotinus in the *Enneads* speaks of the soul's care for the universe: ". . . this all in one universally comprehensive living being, encircling all the living beings within it, and having a soul, one soul which extends to all its members in the degree of participant membership held by each."

Civilization has tamed place. Ground is leveled to build homes and cities. Roads, streets, and floors are level so that we may walk and travel easily. Left to itself, the curvature of the landscape invites presence and the loyalty of stillness. In the distraction of the traveler and the temporary, its ancient thereness goes unnoticed. Humans only know the passing night. Below the surface of landscape the earth lives in the eternal night, the dark and ancient cradle of all origin.

It is no wonder that in the Celtic world, wells were sacred places. Wells were seen as threshold places between the deeper, dark, unknown subterranean world and the outer world of light and form. The land of Ireland was understood in ancient times as the body of the goddess. Wells were reverenced as special apertures through which divinity flowed forth. Manannán mac Lir said, "No one will have knowledge who does not have a drink from the well." Even to this day, people still visit sacred springs. They walk several times around a well, traveling in a clockwise direction, and often leave votive offerings. Different wells are thought to hold different kinds of healing.

When a well awakens in the mind, new possibilities begin to flow, and you find within yourself a depth and excitement that you never knew you had. This art of awakening is suggested by the Irish writer James Stephens, who said,

"The only barrier is our readiness." We often remain exiles, left outside the rich world of the soul, simply because we are not ready. Our task is to refine our hearts and minds. There is so much blessing and beauty near us that is destined for us, and yet it cannot enter our lives because we are not ready to receive it. The handle is on the inside of the door; only we can open it. Our lack of readiness is often caused by blindness, fear, and lack of self-appreciation. When we are ready, we will be blessed. At that moment the door of the heart becomes the gate of heaven. Shakespeare expressed this beautifully in *King Lear:* "Men must endure / Their going hence even as their coming hither; / Ripeness is all."

TO TRANSFIGURE THE EGO—TO LIBERATE THE SOUL

Sometimes our spiritual programs take us far away from our inner belonging. We become addicted to the methods and programs of psychology and religion. We become so desperate to learn how to be, that our lives pass, and we neglect the practice of being. One of the lovely things in the Celtic mind is its sense of spontaneity, which is one of the greatest spiritual gifts. To be spontaneous is to escape the cage of the ego by trusting that which is beyond the self. One of the greatest enemies of spiritual belonging is the ego. The ego does not reflect the real shape of one's individuality. The ego is the false self born out of fear and defensiveness. The ego is a protective crust that we draw around our affections. It is created out of timidity, the failure to trust the Other and to respect our own Otherness. One of the greatest conflicts in life is the conflict between the ego and the soul. The ego is threatened, competitive, and stressed, whereas the soul is drawn more toward surprise, spontaneity, the new and the fresh. Real soul has humor, irony, and no obsessive self-seriousness. It avoids what is weary, worn, or repetitive. The image of the well breaking out of the hard, crusted ground is an illuminating image for the freshness that can suddenly dawn within the heart that remains open to experience.

Freud and Jung illuminated the vast complexity of the soul. The person is no simple, one-dimensional self. There is a labyrinth within the soul. What we think and desire often comes into conflict with what we do. Below the surface of our conscious awareness, a vast, unknown rootage determines our actions. The mythic story of the earth and the gods whispers within us. We become aware of the patterns of blindness and obsession that unknowingly drive us. We find ourselves so often returning to the same empty places that diminish and impoverish our essence. All psychic activity is at first unconscious; this is the realm of concealed wishes.

The unconscious is a powerful and continuous presence. Every life lives out of and struggles with this inner night, which casts its challenging and fecund shadow over everything we do and think and feel. We are earthen vessels that hold the treasure. Yet, aspects of the treasure are darker and more dangerous than we allow ourselves to imagine. When the unconscious becomes illuminated, its darker forces no longer hold us prisoner. This work of freedom is slow and unpredictable; yet it is precisely at this threshold that each individual is the custodian and subject of their own transfiguration. Outside us, society functions in an external way; its collective eye does not know interiority but sees only through the lens of image, impression, and function.

There Is No Spiritual Program

In our time, there is much obsession with spiritual programs. Such spiritual programs tend to be very linear. The spiritual life is imagined as a journey with a sequence of stages. Each stage has its own methodology, negativity, and possibilities. Such a program often becomes an end in itself. It weights our natural presence against us. Such a program can divide and separate us from what is most intimately ours. The past is forsaken as unredeemable, the present is used as the fulcrum to a future that bodes holiness, integration, or perfection. When time is reduced to linear progress, it is emptied of presence. Meister Eckhart radically revises the whole notion of spiritual programs. He says that there is no such thing as a spiritual journey. If a little shocking, this is refreshing. If there were a spiritual journey, it would be only a quarter inch long, though many miles deep. It would be a swerve into rhythm with your deeper nature and presence. The wisdom here is so consoling. You do not have to go away outside yourself to come into real conversation with your soul and with the mysteries of the spiritual world. The eternal is at home—within you.

The eternal is not elsewhere; it is not distant. There is nothing as near as the eternal. This is captured in a lovely Celtic phrase: *"Tá tír na n-óg ar chul an tí—tír álainn trina chéile"*—that is, "The land of eternal youth is behind the house, a beautiful land fluent within itself." The eternal world and the mortal world are not parallel, rather they are fused. The beautiful Gaelic phrase *fighte fuaighte,* "woven into and through each other," captures this.

Behind the facade of our normal lives eternal destiny is shaping our days and our ways. The awakening of the human spirit is a homecoming. Yet ironically our sense of familiarity often militates against our homecoming. When we are familiar with something, we lose the energy, edge, and excitement of it. Hegel said, *"Das Bekannte überhaupt ist darum, weil es bekannt ist, nicht erkannt"*—that is, "Generally, the familiar, precisely because it is familiar, is not known." This is a powerful sentence. Behind the facade of the familiar, strange things await us. This is true of our homes, the place where we live, and, indeed, of those with whom we live. Friendships and relationships suffer immense numbing through the mechanism of familiarization. We reduce the wildness and mystery of person and landscape to the external, familiar image. Yet the familiar is merely a facade. Familiarity enables us to tame, control, and ultimately forget the mystery. We make our peace with the surface as image and we stay away from the Otherness and fecund turbulence of the unknown that it masks. Familiarity is one of the most subtle and pervasive forms of human alienation.

In a book of conversations with P. A. Mendoza, a Colombian writer, Gabriel García Márquez, when asked about his thirty-year relationship with his wife, Mercedes, said, "I know her so well now that I have not the slightest idea who she really is." For Márquez, familiarity is an invitation to adventure and mystery. Conversely, the people close to us have sometimes become so familiar that they have become lost in a distance that no longer invites or surprises. Familiarity can be quiet death, an arrangement that permits the routine to continue without offering any new challenge or nourishment.

This happens also with our experience of place. I remember my first evening in Tübingen, Germany. I was to spend more than four years there studying Hegel, but that first evening Tübingen was utterly strange and unknown to me. I remember thinking, Look very carefully at Tübingen this evening because you will never again see it in the same way. And this was true. After a week there, I knew the way to the lecture halls and seminar rooms, the canteen and library. After I had mapped out my routes through this strange territory, it became familiar, and soon I did not see it for itself anymore.

People have difficulty awakening to their inner world especially when their lives have become overly familiar to them. They find it hard to discover something new, interesting, or adventurous in their numbed lives. Yet everything we need for our journey has already been given to us. Consequently, there is great strangeness in the shadowed light of our soul world. We should become more conversant with our reserved soul-light. The first step in awakening to your inner life and to the depth and promise of your solitude would be to consider yourself for a little while as a stranger to your own deepest depths. To decide to view yourself as a complete stranger, someone who has just stepped ashore in your life, is a liberating exercise. This meditation helps to break the numbing stranglehold of complacency and familiarity. Gradually, you begin to sense the mystery and magic of yourself. You realize that you are not the helpless owner of a deadened life but rather a temporary guest gifted with blessings and possibilities you could neither invent nor earn.

THE BODY IS YOUR ONLY HOME

It is mysterious that the human body is clay. The individual is the meeting place of the four elements. The human person is a clay shape, living in the medium of air. Yet the fire of blood, thought, and soul moves through the body. Its whole life and energy flow in the subtle circle of the water element. We have come up out of the depths of the earth. Consider the millions of continents of clay that will never have the opportunity to leave this underworld. This clay will never find a form to ascend and express itself in the world of light but will live forever in that unknown shadow world. In this regard, the Celtic idea that the underworld is not a dark world but a world of spirit is very beautiful. There is an old belief in Ireland that the Tuatha Dé Dannan, the tribe of Celts banished from the surface of Ireland, now inhabit the underworld beneath the land. From there, they controlled the fecundity of the land above. Consequently, when a king was being crowned, he entered into a symbolic marriage with the goddess. His reign mediated between the visible landscape with its grass, crops, and trees and the hidden subterranean world in which all is rooted. The balance was vital since the Celts were a rural, farming people. This mythological and spiritual perspective has had an immense subconscious effect on how landscape is viewed in Ireland. Landscape is not matter nor merely nature, rather it enjoys a luminosity. Landscape is numinous. Each field has a different name, and in each place something different happened. Landscape has a secret and silent memory, a narrative of presence where nothing is ever lost or forgotten. In Tom Murphy's play *The Gigli Concert*, the unnamed man loses this sense of landscape and simultaneously loses the ability to connect with himself.

The mystery of the Irish landscape is mirrored in all the

stories and legends of different places. There are endless stories about ghosts and spirits. Near us, a magic cat minds
ancient gold in a big field. One finds an enthralling weave of
stories about the independence andf structure of the spiritual
world. The human body has come out of this underworld.
Consequently, in your body, clay is finding a form and shape
that it never found before. Just as it is an immense privilege
for your clay to have come up into the light, it is also a great
responsibility.

In your clay body, things are coming to expression and to
light that were never known before, presences that never came
to light or shape in any other individual. To paraphrase
Heidegger, who said, "Man is a shepherd of being," we could
say, "Man is a shepherd of clay." You represent an unknown
world that begs you to bring it to voice. Often the joy you
feel does not belong to your individual biography but to the
clay out of which you are formed. At other times, you will
find sorrow moving through you, like a dark mist over a landscape. This sorrow is dark enough to paralyze you. It is a mistake to interfere with this movement of feeling. It is more
appropriate to recognize that this emotion belongs more to
your clay than to your mind. It is wise to let this weather of
feeling pass; it is on its way elsewhere. We so easily forget
that our clay has a memory that preceded our minds, a life of
its own before it took its present form. Regardless of how
modern we seem, we still remain ancient, sisters and brothers

of the one clay. In each of us a different part of the mystery becomes luminous. To truly be and become yourself, you need the ancient radiance of others.

Essentially, we belong beautifully to nature. The body knows this belonging and desires it. It does not exile us either spiritually or emotionally. The human body is at home on the earth. It is probably a splinter in the mind that is the sore root of so much of our exile. This tension between clay and mind is the source of all creativity. It is the tension in us between the ancient and the new, the known and the unknown. Only the imagination is native to this rhythm. It alone can navigate in the sublime interim where the lineaments of these differing inner forces touch. The imagination is committed to the justice of wholeness. It will not choose one side in an inner conflict and repress or banish the other; it will endeavor to initiate a profound conversation between them in order that something original can be born. The imagination loves symbol because it recognizes that inner divinity can only find expression in symbolic form. The symbol never gives itself completely to the light. It invites thought precisely because it resides at the threshold of darkness. Through the imagination, the soul creates and constructs your depth experience. Imagination is the most reverent mirror of the inner world.

Individuality need not be lonely or isolated. Cicero said so beautifully, *"Nunquam minus solus quam cum solus."* One can come into harmony with one's individuality if it is viewed as a profound expression or sacrament of the ancient clay. When there is a real awakening in love and friendship, this sense of the clay within can dawn. If you knew the beloved's body well enough, you could imagine where her clay had lain before it came to form in her. You could sense the blend of different tonalities in her clay: Maybe some clay came from beside a calm lake, some from places where nature was exposed and lonely, and more from secluded and reserved places. We never know how many places of nature meet within the human body. Landscape is not all external, some has crept inside the soul. Human presence is infused with landscape.

This profound and numinous presence of nature is brought out in the poem by Amairgen, chief poet of the Milesians, as he steps ashore to take possession of the land on behalf of his people:

> I am the wind which breathes upon the sea,
> I am the wave of the ocean,
> I am the murmur of the billows,
> I am the ox of the seven combats,
> I am the vulture upon the rocks,
> I am a beam of the sun,
> I am the fairest of plants,
> I am the wild boar in valour,
> I am the salmon in the water,
> I am a lake in the plain,

I am a world of knowledge,

I am the point of the lance of battle,

I am the God who created the fire in the head.

(ED. P. MURRAY)

This is traditionally believed to be the first poem ever composed in Ireland. All of the elements of the poem have ruminous associations in early Irish literature. There is no dualism here. All is one. This ancient poem preempts and reverses the lonely helplessness of Descartes's *"cogito ergo sum,"* I think therefore I am. For Amairgen, I am because everything else is. I am in everything and everything is in me. This magnificent hymn to presence outlines the ontological depth and unity of the *anam-ċara* experience.

The Celtic world developed a profound sense of the complexity of the individual. Often the places within us where conflict arises are places where different parts of our clay memory come together; the energy here may at times be unrefined, raw, or difficult. The recognition of our clay nature can bring us a more ancient harmony. It can return us to the ancient rhythm that we inhabited before consciousness made us separate. This is one of the lovely things about the soul. The soul is in the middle ground between the separation of the air and the belonging of the earth. Your soul mediates between your body and your mind; it shelters the two and holds them together. In this primal sense, the soul is imaginative.

The Body Is in the Soul

We must learn to trust the indirect side of our selves. Your soul is the oblique side of your mind and body. Western thought has told us that the soul is in the body. The soul was thought to be confined to some special, small, and refined region within the body. It was often imaged as being white. When a person died, the soul departed and the empty body collapsed. This version of the soul seems false. In fact, the more ancient way of looking at this question considers the relationship of soul to body in a converse way. The body is in the soul. Your soul reaches out farther than your body, and it simultaneously suffuses your body and your mind. Your soul has more refined antennae than your mind or ego. Trusting this more penumbral dimension brings us to new places in the human adventure. But we have to let go in order to be; we have to stop forcing ourselves, or we will never enter our own belonging. There is something ancient at work in us creating novelty. In fact, you need very little in order to develop a real sense of your own spiritual individuality. One of the things that is absolutely essential is silence, the other is solitude.

Solitude is one of the most precious things in the human spirit. It is different from loneliness. When you are lonely, you become acutely conscious of your own separation. Solitude can be a homecoming to your own deepest belonging. One of the lovely things about us as individuals is the incommensurable in us. In each person, there is a point of absolute nonconnection with everything else and with everyone. This is fascinating and frightening. It means that we cannot continue to seek outside ourselves for the things we need from within. The blessings for which we hunger are not to be found in other places or people. These gifts can only be given to you by yourself. They are at home at the hearth of your soul.

To Be Natural Is to Be Holy

In the West of Ireland, many houses have open fires. At wintertime when you visit someone, you go through the bleak and cold landscape until you finally come into the hearth, where the warmth and magic of the fire is waiting. A turf fire is an ancient presence. The turf comes out of the earth and carries the memory of trees and fields and long-gone times. It is strange to have the earth burning within the domesticity of the home. I love the image of the hearth as a place of home, a place of warmth and return.

In everyone's inner solitude there is that bright and warm hearth. The idea of the unconscious, even though it is a very profound and wonderful idea, has sometimes frightened people away from coming back to their own hearth. We falsely understand the subconscious as the cellar where all of our repression and self-damage is housed. Out of our fear of ourselves we have imagined monsters down there. Yeats says,

"Man needs reckless courage to descend into the abyss of himself." In actual fact, these demons do not account for all the subconscious. The primal energy of our soul holds a wonderful warmth and welcome for us. One of the reasons we were sent onto the earth was to make this connection with ourselves, this inner friendship. The demons will haunt us, if we remain afraid. All the classical mythical adventures externalize the demons. In battle with them, the hero always grows, ascending to new levels of creativity and poise. Each inner demon holds a precious blessing that will heal and free you. To receive this gift, you have to lay aside your fear and take the risk of loss and change that every inner encounter offers.

The Celts had a wonderful intuitive understanding of the complexity of the psyche. They believed in various divine presences. Lugh was the god who was most venerated. He was god of light and giftedness. The Shining One. The ancient festival of Lunasa takes its name from him. The earth goddess was Anu, mother of fecundity. They also acknowledged the divine origin of negativity and darkness. There were three mother goddesses of war: Morrigan, Nemain, and Badb. These play a crucial role in *The Tain*, an ancient epic. Gods and goddesses were always linked to place. Trees, wells, and rivers were special places of divine presence. Fostered by such rich textures of divine presence, the ancient psyche was never as isolated and disconnected as the modern psyche. The Celts had an intuitive spirituality informed by mindful and reverent attention to landscape. It was an outdoor spirituality impassioned by the erotic charge of the earth. The recovery of soul in our times is vital in healing our disconnection.

In theological or spiritual terms, we can understand this point of absolute nonconnection with everything as a sacred opening in the soul that can be filled by nothing external. Often all the possessions we have, the work we do, the beliefs we hold, are manic attempts to fill this opening, but they never stay in place. They always slip, and we are left more vulnerable and exposed than before. A time comes when you know that you can no longer wallpaper this void. Until you really listen to the call of this void, you will remain an inner fugitive, driven from refuge to refuge, always on the run with no place to call home. To be natural is to be holy; but it is very difficult to be natural. To be natural is to be at home with your own nature. If you are outside yourself, always reaching beyond yourself, you avoid the call of your own mystery. When you acknowledge the integrity of your solitude and settle into its mystery, your relationships with others take on a new warmth, adventure, and wonder.

Spirituality becomes suspect if it is merely an anaesthetic to still one's spiritual hunger. Such a spirituality is driven by the fear of loneliness. If you bring courage to your solitude, you learn that you do not need to be afraid. The phrase "do not be afraid" recurs 366 times in the Bible. There is a welcome for you at the heart of your solitude. When you realize this, most of the fear that governs your life falls away. The moment your fear transfigures, you come into rhythm with your own self.

THE DANCING MIND

There are many different kinds of solitude. There is the solitude of suffering, when you go through darkness that is lonely, intense, and terrible. Words become powerless to express your pain; what others hear from your words is so distant and different from what you are actually suffering. Everyone goes through that bleak time. Folk-consciousness always recognizes that at such a time, you must be exceedingly gentle with yourself. I love the image of the field of corn in the autumn. When the wind catches the corn, it does not stand stiff and direct against the force of the wind; were it to do this, the wind would rip it asunder. No. The corn weaves with the wind, it bends low. And when the wind is gone, it weaves back and finds its own poise and balance again. There is also the lovely story of the wolf-spider, which never builds its web between two hard objects like two stones. If it did this, the web would be rent by the wind. Instinctively, it builds its web between two blades of grass. When the wind comes, the web lowers with the grass until the wind has passed, then it comes back up and finds its point of balance and equilibrium again. These are beautiful images for a mind in rhythm with itself. We put terrible pressure on our minds.

When we tighten them or harden our views or beliefs, we lose all the softness and flexibility that makes for real shelter, belonging, and protection. Sometimes the best way of caring for your soul is to make flexible again some of the views that harden and crystalize your mind; for these alienate you from your own depth and beauty. Creativity seems to demand flexible and measured tension. In musical terms, the image of the violin is instructive here. If the strings are tuned too tightly they snap. When the tuning is balanced, the violin can endure massive force and produce the most powerful and tender music.

BEAUTY LIKES NEGLECTED PLACES

Only in solitude can you discover a sense of your own beauty. The Divine Artist sent no one here without the depth and light of divine beauty. This beauty is frequently concealed behind the dull facade of routine. Only in your solitude will you come upon your own beauty. In Connemara, where there are a lot of fishing villages, there is a phrase that says, "*Is fánach an áit a gheobfá gliomach*"—that is, "It is in the unexpected or neglected place that you will find the lobster." In the neglected crevices and corners of your evaded solitude, you will find the treasure that you have always sought elsewhere. Ezra Pound said something similar about beauty: Beauty likes to keep away from the public glare. It likes to find a neglected or abandoned place, for it knows that it is only here it will meet the kind of light that repeats its shape, dignity, and nature. There is a deep beauty within each person. Modern culture is obsessed with cosmetic perfection. Beauty is standardized; it has become another product for sale. In its real sense, beauty is the illumination of your soul.

There is a lantern in the soul, which makes your solitude luminous. Solitude need not remain lonely. It can awaken to its luminous warmth. The soul redeems and transfigures everything because the soul is the divine space. When you inhabit your solitude fully and experience its outer extremes of isolation and abandonment, you will find that at its heart there is neither loneliness nor emptiness but intimacy and shelter. In your solitude you are frequently nearer to the heart of belonging and kinship than you are in your social life or public world. At this level, memory is the great friend of solitude. The harvest of memory opens when solitude is ripe. This is captured succinctly by Wordsworth in his response to the memory of the daffodils: "Oft when on my couch I lie / In vacant or pensive mood / They flash upon the inward eye / Which is the bliss of solitude."

Your persona, beliefs, and role are in reality a technique or strategy for getting through the daily routine. When you are on your own, or when you wake in the middle of the night, the real knowing within you can surface. You come to feel the secret equilibrium of your soul. When you travel the inner distance and reach the divine, the outer distance vanishes.

Ironically, your trust in your inner belonging radically alters your outer belonging. Unless you find belonging in your solitude, your external longing will remain needy and driven.

There is a wonderful welcome within. Meister Eckhart illuminates this point. He says that there is a place in the soul that neither space nor time nor flesh can touch. This is the eternal place within us. It would be a lovely gift to yourself to go there often—to be nourished, strengthened, and renewed. The deepest things that you need are not elsewhere. They are here and now in that circle of your own soul. Real friendship and holiness enable a person to frequently visit the hearth of his solitude; this benediction invites an approach to others in their blessedness.

THOUGHTS ARE OUR INNER SENSES

Our life in the world comes to us in the shape of time. Consequently, our expectation is both a creative and constructive force. If you expect to find nothing within yourself but the repressed, abandoned, and shameful elements of your past or a haunted hunger, all you will find is emptiness and desperation. If you do not bring the kind eye of creative expectation to your inner world, you will never find anything there. The way you look at things is the most powerful force in shaping your life. In a vital sense, perception is reality.

Phenomenology has shown us that all consciousness is

consciousness *of* something. The world is never simply there outside us. Our intentionality constructs it. For the most part, we construct our world so naturally that we are unaware that we are doing this every moment. It seems that the same rhythm of construction works inwardly, too. Our intentionality constructs the landscapes of our inner world. Maybe it is time now for a phenomenology of soul. The soul creates, shapes, and peoples our inner life. The gateway to our deepest identity is not through mechanical analysis. We need to listen to the soul and articulate its wisdom in a poetic and mystical form. It is tempting to use the soul as merely another receptacle for our tired and frustrated analytical energies. It deserves to be remembered that from ancient times the soul had depth, danger, and unpredictability precisely because it was seen as the presence of the divine within us. If we cut the soul off from the Holy, it becomes an innocuous cipher. To awaken the soul is also to travel to the frontier where experience bows down before the *mysterium tremendum et fascinans* of Otherness.

There is such an intimate connection between the way we look at things and what we actually discover. If you can learn to look at yourself and your life in a gentle, creative, and adventurous way, you will be eternally surprised at what you find. In other words, we never meet anything totally or purely. We see everything through the lens of thought. The way that you think determines what you will actually discover. This is expressed wonderfully by Meister Eckhart: "Thoughts are our inner senses." We know that when our outer senses are impaired, this immediately diminishes the presence of the world to us. If your sight is poor, the world becomes a blur. If your hearing is damaged, a dull silence replaces what could be music or the voice of your beloved. In a similar way, if your thoughts are impaired or if they are negative or diminished, then you will never discover anything rich or beautiful within your soul. If thoughts are our inner senses, and if we allow our thoughts to be impoverished and pale, then the riches of our inner world can never come to meet us. We have to imagine more courageously if we are to greet creation more fully.

You relate to your inner world through thought. If these thoughts are not your own thoughts, then they are secondhand thoughts. Each of us needs to learn the unique language of our own soul. In that distinctive language, we will discover a lens of thought to brighten and illuminate our inner world. Dostoyevsky said that many people lived their lives without ever finding themselves in themselves. If you are afraid of your solitude, or if you only meet your solitude with entrenched or impoverished thought, you will never enter your own depth. It is a great point of growth in your life when you allow what is luminous within to awaken you. This may be the first time that you actually see yourself as you are. The mystery of your presence can never be reduced to your role, actions, ego, or image. You are an eternal essence; this is the ancient reason why you are here. To begin to get a glimpse of this essence is to come into harmony with your destiny and with the providence that always minds your days and ways. This process of self-discovery is not easy; it may involve suffering, doubt, dismay. But we must not shrink from the fullness of our being in attempting to reduce the pain.

ASCETIC SOLITUDE

Ascetic solitude is difficult. You withdraw from the world to get a clearer glimpse of who you are, what you are doing, and where life is taking you. The people who do this in a very committed way are the contemplatives. When you visit someone at home, the door into the house, the threshold, is rich with the textures of presence from all the welcomes and valedictions that have occurred on that threshold. When you visit a cloister or contemplative convent, no one meets you at the door. You go in, ring a bell, and the person arrives behind the grille to meet you. These are the special houses that hold the survivors of solitude. They have exiled themselves from the outside worship of the earth to risk themselves in the interior space where the senses have nothing to celebrate.

Ascetic solitude involves silence. And silence is one of the great victims of modern culture. We live in an intense and visually aggressive age; everything is drawn outward toward the sensation of the image. A consequence of culture becoming ever more homogenized and universalist is that image has such power. With the continued netting of everything, chosen images can immediately attain universality. There is an incredibly subtle and powerfully calculating industry of modern dislocation, where that which is deep and lives in the silence within us is completely ignored. The surfaces of our minds continue to be seduced by the power of images. There is a sinister eviction taking place; peoples' lives are being dragged outward all the time. The inner world of the soul is suffering a great eviction by the landlord forces of advertising and external social reality. This outer exile really impoverishes us. One of the reasons so many people are suffering from stress is not that they are doing stressful things but that they allow so little time for silence. A fruitful solitude without silence and space is inconceivable.

Silence is one of the major thresholds in the world. The spirituality of the Desert Fathers deeply influenced Celtic spirituality. For these ascetics, silence was the teacher: "A certain brother came to the abbott Moses in Scete seeking a word from him. And the old man said to him, 'Go and sit in your cell, and your cell will teach you all things.'" In the Celtic world there was always the recognition of the silent and the unknown as the closest companions of the human journey. Encounter and farewell, which framed conversations, were always blessings. Emer gives a lovely blessing to Cúchulainn in *The Taín*. She says, "May your road be blessed," literally, I drive around you in a chariot turning to the right. This was the sun's direction and it attracted good fortune. Behind Celtic poetry and prayer is the sense that the words have emerged from a deep, reverential silence. This perspective of solitude and silence purified and intensified the encounter of two people in the *anam-ċara* experience.

Fundamentally, there is the great silence that meets language; all words come out of silence. Words that have a depth, resonance, healing, and challenge to them are words loaded with ascetic silence. Language that does not recognize its kinship with reality is banal, denotative, and purely discursive. The language of poetry issues from and returns to silence. In modern culture, conversation is one of the casualties. Usually when you talk to people, all you hear is surface narrative or the catalog of therapy news. It is quite poignant to hear people describe themselves in terms of the program in which they are involved or the outer work that their role involves.

Each person is the daily recipient of new thoughts and unexpected feelings. Yet so often in our social encounters and in the way we have grown used to describing ourselves, these thoughts and feelings are not welcome and remain unexpressed. This is disappointing in view of the fact that the deepest things that we have inherited have come down to us across the bridges of meaningful conversation. The Celtic tradition was primarily an oral tradition. The stories, poems, and prayers lived for centuries in the memory and voice of the people. They were learned by heart. The companionship and presence of such a rich harvest of memory helped poeticize their perception and conversation. Without the presence of memory conversation becomes amnesic, repetitive, and superficial. Perception is most powerful when it engages both memory and experience. This empowers conversation to become real exploration. Real conversation has an unpredictability, danger, and resonance; it can take a turn anywhere and constantly borders on the unexpected and on the unknown. Real conversation is not a construct of the solitary ego; it creates community. So much of our modern talk is like a spider weaving a web of language maniacally outside itself. Our parallel monologues with their staccato stutter only reinforce our isolation. There is so little patience for the silence from which words emerge or for the silence that is between words and within them. When we forget or neglect this silence, we empty our world of its secret and subtle presences. We can no longer converse with the dead or the absent.

SILENCE IS THE SISTER OF THE DIVINE

Meister Eckhart said that there is nothing in the world that resembles God so much as silence. Silence is a great friend of the soul; it unveils the riches of solitude. It is very difficult to reach that quality of inner silence. You must make a space for it so that it may begin to work for you. In a certain sense, you do not need the whole armory and vocabulary of therapies, psychologies, or spiritual programs. If you have a trust in and an expectation of your own solitude, everything that you need to know will be revealed to you. These are some wonderful lines from the French poet René Char: "Intensity is silent, its image is not. I love everything that dazzles me and then accentuates the darkness within me." Here is an image of silence as the force that discloses hidden depth. Silence is the sister of the divine.

One of the tasks of true friendship is to listen compassionately and creatively to the hidden silences. Often secrets are not revealed in words, they lie concealed in the silence between the words or in the depth of what is unsayable between two people. In modern life there is an immense rush to expression. Sometimes the quality of what is expressed is superficial and immensely repetitive. A greater tolerance of silence is desirable, that fecund silence, which is the source of our most resonant language. The depth and substance of a friendship mirrors itself in the quality and shelter of the silence between two people.

As you begin to befriend your inner silence, one of the first things you will notice is the superficial chatter on the surface level of your mind. Once you recognize this, the silence deepens. A distinction begins to emerge between the images that you have of yourself and your own deeper nature. Sometimes much of the conflict in our spirituality has nothing to do with our deeper nature but rather with the false surface constructs we build. We then get caught in working out a grammar and geometry of how these surface images and positions relate to each other; meanwhile our deeper nature remains unattended.

THE CROWD AT THE HEARTH OF THE SOUL

Individuality is never simple or one-dimensional. Often it seems as if there is a crowd within the individual heart. The Greeks believed that when you dreamed at night, the figures of your dreams were characters who left your body, went out into the world, and undertook their own adventures; they then returned before you awoke. At the deepest level of the human heart, there is no simple, singular self. Deep within, there is a gallery of different selves. Each one of these figures expresses a different part of your nature. Sometimes they will come into contradiction and conflict with each other. If you meet these contradictions only on the surface level, this can start an inner feud that could haunt you all the days of your life. Frequently, you see people who are sorely divided. They are in a permanent war zone and have never managed to go deeper to the hearth of kinship, where the two forces are not enemies but reveal themselves as different sides of the one belonging.

We cannot embody in action the multiplicity of selves we encounter in our most inward meditations. But without a knowledge of these numberless selves, our existence is severely diminished and our access to mystery is blocked. We are talking here of the imagination and its riches; too often we degrade imagination to a problem-solving technique.

We need to develop a new sense of the wonderful complexity of the self. We need thought models or patterns that are fair and appropriate to that complexity. When people discover their own complexity, they become afraid, and with the hammers of secondhand thoughts they beat this rich internal landscape into a monoscape. They make themselves conform. They agree to fit in; they cease to be vivid presences, even to themselves.

CONTRADICTIONS AS TREASURES

One of the most interesting forms of complexity is contradiction. We need to rediscover contradiction as a creative force within the soul. Beginning with Aristotle, the Western thought tradition outlawed contradiction as the presence of the impossible, and consequently, as an index of the false and the illogical. Hegel, alone, had the vision, subtlety, and hospitality of reflection to acknowledge contradiction as the complex force of growth that disavows mere linear progress in order to awaken all the aggregate energies of an experience. It is the turbulence and conflict of their inner conversation that brings an integrity of transfiguration and not the mere replacement of one image, surface, or system by another, which so often passes for change. This perspective makes for a more complex notion of truth. It demands an ethic of authenticity that incorporates and goes beyond the simplistic intentions of mere sincerity.

We need to have greater patience with our sense of inner contradiction in order to allow its different dimensions to come into conversation within us. There is a secret light and vital energy in contradiction. Where there is energy there is life and growth. Your ascetic solitude will allow your contradictions to emerge with clarity and force. If you remain faithful to this energy, you will gradually come to participate in a harmony that lies deeper than any contradiction. This will give you new courage to engage the depth, danger, and darkness of your life.

It is startling that we desperately hold on to what makes us miserable. Our own woundedness becomes a source of perverse pleasure and fixes our identity. We do not want to be cured, for that would mean moving into the unknown. Often it seems we are destructively addicted to the negative. What we call the negative is usually the surface form of contradiction. If we maintain our misery at this surface level, we hold off the initially threatening but ultimately redemptive and healing transfiguration that comes through engaging our inner contradiction. We need to revalue what we consider to be negative. Rilke used to say that difficulty is one of the greatest friends of the soul. Our lives would be immeasurably enriched if we could but bring the same hospitality in meeting the negative as we bring to the joyful and pleasurable. In avoiding the negative, we only encourage it to recur. We need a new way of understanding and integrating the negative. The negative is one of the closest friends of your destiny. It contains essential energies that you need and that you cannot find elsewhere. This is where art can be so illuminating. Art is full of intimations of the negative in ways that allow you to participate imaginatively in their possibility. The experience of art can help you build a creative friendship with the negative. When you stand before a painting by Kandinsky, you enter the church of color where the liturgy of contradiction is fluent and glorious. When you listen to Martha Argerich play Rachmaninov's *Piano Concerto No. 3 in D Minor, Op. 30*, you experience the liberation of contradictory forces that at every point threaten and test the magnificent symmetry of form that holds them.

You can only befriend the negative if you recognize that it is not destructive. It often seems that morality is the enemy of growth. We falsely understand moral rules as descriptions of the soul's direction and duty. Yet the best thinking in moral philosophy tells us that these rules are only signposts to alert us to the complex of values latent in or consequent upon our decisions. Moral rules encourage us to act with honor, compassion, and justice. They can never be descriptions simply because each person and situation is so different. When we notice something immoral, we normally tend to be harsh with ourselves and employ moral surgery to remove it. In doing this, we are only ensuring that it remains trapped within. We merely confirm our negative view of ourselves and ignore our potential for growth. There is a strange paradox in the soul: If you try to avoid or remove the awkward quality, it will pursue you. In fact, the only effective way to still its unease is to transfigure it, to let it become something creative and positive that contributes to who you are.

One encouraging aspect of the negative is its truthfulness. The negative does not lie. It will tell you clearly where you court absence rather than inhabit presence. On entering your solitude, one of the first presences to announce itself is the negative. Nietzsche said that one of the best days in his life was the day when he rebaptized all his negative qualities as his best qualities. In this kind of baptism, rather than banishing what is at first glimpse unwelcome, you bring it home to unity with your life. This is the slow and difficult work of self-retrieval. Every person has certain qualities or presences in their heart that are awkward, disturbing, and negative. One of your sacred duties is to exercise kindness toward them. In a sense, you are called to be a loving parent to your delinquent qualities. Your kindness will slowly poultice their negativity, alleviate their fear, and help them to see that your soul is a home where there is no judgment or febrile hunger for a fixed and limited identity. The negative threatens us so powerfully precisely because it is an invitation to an art of compassion and self-enlargement that our small thinking utterly resists. Your vision is your home, and your home should have many mansions to shelter your wild divinity. Such integration respects the multiplicity of selves within. It does not force them into a factitious unity, it allows them to cohere as one, each bringing its unique difference to complement the harmony.

This rhythm of self-retrieval invites your generosity and sense of risk, not merely internally, but also externally, at the interpersonal level. This is probably the uneasy territory of which Jesus spoke when he exhorted, Love your enemies. We should be careful in our choice of "adversaries." An awakened soul should have only worthy "adversaries" who reveal your negativity and challenge your possibility. To learn to love your adversaries is to earn a freedom that is beyond resentment and threat.

THE SOUL ADORES UNITY

When you decide to practice inner hospitality, the self-torment ceases. The abandoned, neglected, and negative selves come into a seamless unity. The soul is wise and subtle; it recognizes that unity fosters belonging. The soul adores unity. What you separate, the soul joins. As your experience extends and deepens, your memory becomes richer and more complex. Your soul is the priestess of memory, selecting, sifting, and ultimately gathering your vanishing days toward presence. This liturgy of remembrance, literally re-membering, is always at work within you. Human solitude is rich and endlessly creative.

The solitude of nature is mainly silent. This is expressed beautifully in an old Irish wisdom: *"Castar na daoine ar a chéile ach ní castar na sléibhte ar a chéile"*—that is, "The mountains never meet, but people can always encounter each other." It is strange that two mountains can be side by side for millions of years and yet can never move closer to each other. Whereas two strangers can come down these mountains, meet in the valley, and share the inner worlds they carry. This separation must be one of nature's loneliest experiences.

The ocean is one of the delights for the human eye. The seashore is a theater of fluency. When the mind is entangled, it is soothing to walk by the seashore, to let the rhythm of the ocean inside you. The ocean disentangles the netted mind. Everything loosens and comes back to itself. The false divisions are relieved, released, and healed. Yet the ocean never actually sees itself. Even light, which enables us to see everything, cannot see itself; light is blind. In Haydn's *Creation* it is the vocation of man and woman to celebrate and complete creation.

Our solitude is different. In contrast to nature and to the animal world, there is a mirror within the human mind. This mirror collects every reflection. Human solitude is so unsolitary. Deep human solitude is a place of great affinity and of tension. When you come into your solitude, you come into companionship with everything and everyone. When you extend yourself frenetically outward, seeking refuge in your external image or role, you are going into exile. When you come patiently and silently home to yourself, you come into unity and into belonging.

No one but you can sense the eternity and depth concealed in your solitude. This is one of the lonely things about individuality. You arrive at a sense of the eternal in you only through confronting and outfacing your fears. The truly lonely element in loneliness is fear. No one else has access to the world you carry around within yourself; you are its custodian and entrance. No one else can see the world the way you see it. No one else can feel your life the way you feel it. Thus it is impossible to ever compare two people because each stands on such different ground. When you compare yourself to others, you are inviting envy into your consciousness; it can be a dangerous and destructive guest. This is always one of the great tensions in an awakened or spiritual life, namely, to find the rhythm of its unique language, perception, and belonging. To remain faithful to your life requires commitment and vision that must be constantly renewed.

If you try to view yourself through the lenses that others offer you, all you will see are distortions; your own light and beauty will become blurred, awkward, and ugly. Your sense of inner beauty has to remain a very private thing. The secret and the sacred are sisters. Our times suffer from such a loss of the sacred because our respect for the secret has completely vanished. Our modern technology of information is one of the great destroyers of privacy. We need to shelter that which is deep and reserved within us. This is why there is such hunger in modern life for the language of the soul. The soul is a shy presence. The hunger for the language of the soul shows that the soul has been forced to recede to private areas; only there can it mind its own texture and rhythm. The modern world, by trumpeting the doctrine of self-sufficiency, has denied the soul and forced it to eke out its existence on the margins.

Maybe one of the ways to reconnect with your deeper soul-life is to recover a sense of the soul's shyness. Though it may be personally difficult to be shy, it is an attractive quality in a person. In an unexpected piece of advice, Nietzsche says one of the best ways to make someone interested in you is to blush. The value of shyness, its mystery and reserve, is alien to the brash immediacy of many modern encounters. If we are to connect with our inner life, we need to learn not to grasp at the soul in a direct or confrontational way. In other words, the neon consciousness of much modern psychology and spirituality will always leave us in soul poverty.

Toward a Spirituality of Noninterference

On a farm you learn to respect nature, particularly for the wisdom of its dark underworld. When you sow things in the spring, you commit them to the darkness of the soil. The soil does its own work. It is destructive to interfere with the rhythm and wisdom of its darkness. You sow drills of potatoes on Tuesday and you are delighted with them. You meet someone on a Wednesday who says that you spread the potatoes too thickly, you will have no crop. You dig up the potatoes again and spread them more thinly. On the following Monday, you meet an agricultural advisor who says this particular variety of seed potatoes needs to be spread close together. You dig them up again and set them closer to each other. If you keep scraping at the garden, you will never allow anything to grow. People in our hungry modern world are always scraping at the clay of their hearts. They have a new thought, a new plan, a new syndrome, that now explains why they are the way they are. They have found an old memory that opens a new wound. They keep on relentlessly, again and again, scraping the clay away from their own hearts. In nature we do not see the trees, for instance, getting seriously involved in therapeutic analysis of their root systems or the whole stony world that they had to avoid on their way to the light. Each tree grows in two directions at once, into the darkness and out to the light with as many branches and roots as it needs to embody its wild desires.

Negative introspection damages the soul. It holds many people trapped for years and years, and ironically, it never allows them to change. It is wise to allow the soul to carry on its secret work in the night side of your life. You might not see anything stirring for a long time. You might have only the slightest intimations of the secret growth that is happening within you, but these intimations are sufficient. We should be fulfilled and satisfied with them. You cannot dredge the depths of the soul with the meagre light of self-analysis. The inner world never reveals itself cheaply. Perhaps analysis is the wrong way to approach our inner dark.

We all have wounds; we need to attend to them and allow them to heal. A beautiful phrase of Hegel's is apposite here: "*Die Wunden des Geistes heilen, ohne dass Narben bleiben*"; "The wounds of the spirit heal and leave no scars." There is a healing for each of our wounds, but this healing is waiting in the indirect, oblique, and nonanalytic side of our nature. We need to be mindful of where we are damaged, then invite our deeper soul in its night-world to heal this wounded tissue, renew us, and bring us back into unity. If we approach our hurt indirectly and kindly, it will heal. Creative expectation brings you healing and renewal. If you could trust your soul, you would receive every blessing you require. Life itself is the great sacrament through which we are wounded and healed. If we live everything, life will be faithful to us.

ONE OF THE GREATEST SINS IS THE UNLIVED LIFE

In the Western tradition, we were taught many things about the nature of negativity and the nature of sin, but we were never told that one of the greatest sins is the unlived life. We are sent into the world to live to the full everything that awakens within us and everything that comes toward us. It is a lonely experience to be at the deathbed of someone who is full of regret; to hear him say how he would love another year to do the things his heart had always dreamed of but believed he could never do until he retired. He had always postponed the dream of his heart. There are many people who do not live the lives they desire. Many of the things that hold them back from inhabiting their destiny are false. These are only images in their minds. They are not real barriers at all. We should never allow our fears or the expectations of others to set the frontiers of our destiny.

We are so privileged to still have time. We have but one life, and it is a shame to limit it by fear and false barriers. Irenaeus, a wonderful philosopher and theologian in the second century, said, "The glory of God is the human person fully alive." It is lovely to imagine that real divinity is the presence in which all beauty, unity, creativity, darkness, and negativity are harmonized. The divine has such passionate creativity and instinct for the fully inhabited life. If you allow yourself to be the person that you are, then everything will come into rhythm. If you live the life you love, you will receive shelter and blessings. Sometimes the great famine of blessing in and around us derives from the fact that we are not living the life we love, rather we are living the life that is expected of us. We have fallen out of rhythm with the secret signature and light of our own nature.

The shape of each soul is different. There is a secret destiny for each person. When you endeavor to repeat what others have

done or force yourself into a preset mold, you betray your individuality. We need to return to the solitude within, to find
again the dream that lies at the hearth of the soul. We need to
feel the dream with the wonder of a child approaching a threshold of discovery. When we rediscover our childlike nature, we
enter into a world of gentle possibility. Consequently, we will
find ourselves more frequently at that place, at the place of ease,
delight, and celebration. The false burdens fall away. We come
into rhythm with ourselves. Our clay shape gradually learns to
walk beautifully on this magnificent earth.

A Blessing of Solitude

May you recognize in your life the presence, power, and light
of your soul.
May you realize that you are never alone,
that your soul in its brightness and belonging connects you
intimately with the rhythm of the universe.
May you have respect for your own individuality and
difference.
May you realize that the shape of your soul is unique, that
you have a special destiny here,
that behind the facade of your life there is something
beautiful, good, and eternal happening.
May you learn to see yourself with the same delight, pride,
and expectation with which God sees you in every moment.

FOUR

WORK AS A POETICS OF GROWTH

THE EYE CELEBRATES MOTION

The human eye adores movement and is alert to the slightest flicker. It enjoys great moments of celebration when it beholds the ocean as the tide comes in, and tide upon tide repeats its dance against the shore. The eye also loves the way light moves, summer light behind a cloud crawling over a meadow. The eye follows the way the wind shovels leaves and sways trees. The human is always attracted to motion. As a little baby, you wanted to crawl, then to walk, and as an adult you feel the continuous desire to walk into independence and freedom.

Everything alive is in movement. This movement we call growth. The most exciting form of growth is not mere physical growth but the inner growth of one's soul and life. It is here that the holy longing within the heart brings one's life into motion. The deepest wish of the heart is that this motion does not remain broken or jagged but develops sufficient fluency to become the rhythm of one's life.

The secret heart of time is change and growth. Each new experience that awakens in you adds to your soul and deepens your memory. The person is always a nomad, journeying from threshold to threshold, into ever different experiences. In each new experience, another dimension of the soul unfolds. It is no wonder that from ancient times the human has been understood as a wanderer. Traditionally, these wanderers traversed foreign territories and unknown places. Yet Stanislavsky, the Russian dramatist and thinker, said that "the longest and most exciting journey is the journey inwards."

There is a beautiful complexity of growth within the human soul. In order to glimpse this, it is helpful to visualize the mind as a tower of windows. Sadly, many people remain trapped at the one window, looking out every day at the same scene in the same way. Real growth is experienced when you draw back from that one window, turn, and walk around the inner tower of the soul and see all the different windows that await your gaze. Through these different windows, you can see new vistas of possibility, presence, and creativity. Complacency, habit, and blindness often prevent you from feeling your life. So much depends on the frame of vision—the window through which you look.

TO GROW IS TO CHANGE

In a poetics of growth it is important to explore how possibility and change remain so faithful to us. They open us to new depths within. Their continual, inner movement makes us aware of the eternity that hides behind the outer facade of our lives. Deep within every life, no matter how dull or ineffectual it may seem from the outside, there is something eternal happening. This is the secret way that change and possibility conspire with growth. John Henry Newman summed this up beautifully when he said, "To grow is to change and to be perfect is to have changed often." Change, therefore, need not be threatening; it can in fact bring our lives to perfection. Perfection is not cold completion. Neither is it avoidance of risk and danger in order to keep the soul pure or the conscience unclouded. When you are faithful to the risk and ambivalence of growth, you are engaging your life. The soul loves risk; it is only through the door of risk that growth can enter. Hölderlin wrote,

Nah ist
Und schwer zu fassen der Gott.
Wo aher Gefahr ist, wächst
Das Rettende auch.

Near is
and difficult to understand the God
But where danger is
The redemptive also grows.

Possibility and change become growth within the shape of time that we call a day. Days are where we live. This rhythm shapes our lives. Your life takes the form of each new day that is given to you. The wonderful Polish poet Tadeusz Różewicz describes the difficulty of writing good poetry. A writer writes and writes and writes, and yet the harvest is so minimal. Nonetheless, Różewicz quotes an old dictum that says, "It is more difficult to spend a day well than to write a book." A day is precious because each day is essentially the microcosm of your whole life. Each new day offers possibilities and promises that were never seen before. To engage with honor the full possibility of your life is to engage in a worthy way the possibility of your new day. Each day is different. In the Book of Revelation, God said, "The world of the past has gone. . . . Behold I am making all of creation new." The new day deepens what has already happened and unfolds what is surprising, unpredictable, and creative. You may wish to change your life, you may be in therapy or religion, but your new vision remains merely talk until it enters the practice of your day.

THE CELTIC REVERENCE FOR THE DAY

Celtic spirituality has a great sense of the significance of each day, how the new day is sacred. The Celts never entered the day with a repetitious deadening perspective; they took each day as a new beginning. A lovely Celtic prayer articulates this sense of the day as a gift from God. The metaphor of vision suffuses the poem. There is an invocation that the human eye may "bless all it sees" and that God's vision may guard and guide the day. The day is understood as a time of reflexive blessing that embraces God, self, others, and nature.

> God bless to me the new day
> never vouchsaved to me before
> it is to bless thy own presence thou has given triumph
> God.
> Bless thou to me mine eye
> may mine eye bless all it sees
> I will bless my neighbor
> may my neighbor bless me,
> God give me a clean heart
> let me not from sight of thine eye
> bless to me my children and my wife
> and bless to me my means and cattle.
>
> (TRANS. A. CARMICHAEL)

For the Celtic person the new day was lived amidst nature. It is easy to have a creative sense of the day when you live in the presence of the great divinity called nature. For the Celtic people, nature was not matter, rather it was a luminous and numinous presence that had depth, possibility, and beauty.

There is also a beautiful invocation of the day in an ancient poem called "The Deer's Cry":

I arise today

Through God's strength to direct me,

God's might to uphold me,

God's wisdom to guide me,

God's eye to look before,

God's ear to hear me,

God's word to speak to me,

God's hand to guard me,

God's way to lie before me,

God's shield to protect me.

God's hosts to save me from snares of devils

From temptation of vices,

From everyone who shall wish me ill,

Afar and anear,

Alone and in a multitude.

(TRANS. KUNO MEYER)

This poem articulates the Celtic recognition of the omnipresence of God. The very act of awakening is recognized as a gift. At the threshold of a new day there is no arrogance; rather, a longing to praise. God is pictured in sensuous detail as the divine *anam čara*. At every moment and in every situation, God is the intimate, attentive, and encouraging friend.

This notion of the day as a sacred place offers a lovely frame for the creativity that a day can bring. Your life becomes the shape of the days you inhabit. Days enter us. Sadly, in modern life, the day is often a cage where a person can lose youthfulness, energy, and strength. The day is often experienced as a cage precisely because it is spent in the workplace. So many of our days and so much of our time is spent doing work that remains outside the territories of creativity and feeling. Negotiating the workplace can be complex and very difficult. Most of us work for someone else and lose so much of our energy. As a matter of fact, one of the definitions of energy is the ability to do work. Days spent caged make us tired and weary. In a city, all the morning traffic jams hold people who are barely out of the night and are sleepy, anxious, and frustrated. Pressure and stress have already stolen their day. In the evening, the same people are weary after a long workday. By the time they get home, they have no energy left to the desires, thoughts, and feelings that were neglected all day.

It is very difficult, at first consideration, to bring the world of work and the world of soul together. Most of us work in order to survive. We need to make money; we have no choice. On the other hand, those who are unemployed feel frustrated and demeaned and suffer a great loss of dignity. Yet those of us who work are often caught within a grid of predictability and repetition. It is the same every day. There is such an anonymous side to work. All that is demanded of us is the input of our energy. We move through the workplace, and as soon as we are gone in the evening, we are forgotten. We often feel that our contribution, while it is required and demanded, is merely functional and in reality hardly appreciated. Work should not be like that at all; it should be an arena of possibility and real expression.

THE SOUL DESIRES EXPRESSION

The human deeply desires expression. One of the most beautiful ways the soul is present is through thought. Thoughts are the forms of the soul's inner swiftness. In a certain sense, there is nothing in the world as swift as a thought. It can fly anywhere and be with anyone. Our feelings too can move swiftly; yet even though they are precious to our own identity, thoughts and feelings still remain largely invisible. In order to feel real, we need to bring that inner invisible world to expression. Every life needs the possibility of expression.

When we perform an action, the invisible within us finds a form and comes to expression. Therefore, our work should be the place where the soul can enjoy becoming visible and present. The rich unknown, reserved and precious within us, can emerge into visible form. Our nature longs deeply for the possibility of expression in what we call work.

I was raised on a farm. We were poor, and each of us had to do our share of work. I am always grateful that I was taught how to work. Ever since, I have found satisfaction in being able to do a day's work. I find it frustrating when a day goes astray and at evening I sense that many of the possibilities that slept in that day remained unmet. On a farm, work has a clear and visible effect. When you are digging potatoes, you see the results of your harvesting; the garden yields its buried, nurtured fruit. When you build a wall in a field, you are introducing a new presence into the landscape. If you are out footing turf on the bog, in the evening you see all the *gro-gain* of turf standing up ready to dry. There is great satisfaction in farmwork. Even though it is difficult, you still see a great return for your work. When I left home, I entered the world of thought, writing, and poetry. This work is in the invisible realm. When you work in the territory of mind, you see nothing. Only sometimes are you given the slightest little glimpse of the ripples from your effort. You need great patience and self-trust to sense the invisible harvest in the territory of the mind. You need to train the inner eye for the invisible realms where thoughts can grow, and where feelings put down their roots.

PISREOGA

For many people, the workplace is unsatisfactory and permits neither growth nor creativity. More often than not, it is an anonymous place where function and image have control. Since work demands such labor and effort, it has always made the worker vulnerable. Even in the ancient Celtic tradition, negativity could be harnessed to make nature work against the worker. When people disliked each other or wanted to damage each other, they often did it through destroying that person's harvest. This is the world of *pisreoga*. Maybe one neighbor was jealous of another and planted eggs in his garden of potatoes. When the neighbor goes to dig up the potatoes at harvesttime, the potatoes have decayed. The destructive wish of the neighbor is realized through a ritual of negative invocation and the symbol of an egg. This then robs the power and the fruitfulness of the garden.

In the Celtic tradition, the first of May was a precarious date. The Celts guarded their wells at this time; negative or destructive spirits might want to destroy, poison, or damage them. Such negativity is illustrated in a story my uncle used to tell of a neighboring village. One May morning, a farmer was out herding his animals. He met a strange woman pulling a rope along the meadow. He greeted her by saying a blessing: *"Dia Dhuit."* But she did not answer. Rather, she turned and disappeared, leaving the rope behind her. It was a fine rope. He coiled it and brought it back to the house and threw it into a barrel in one of the outhouses, where it lay forgotten. The following harvest, the neighbors were helping him bring hay home from the meadows with the horse and cart and they needed an extra rope to tie the load of hay. Someone asked if he had any other rope. He said, *"Níl aon rópa agam ach rópa an t-sean cailleach"*—that is, "I have no rope but the rope of the old hag." He went to the shed to find the rope, but when he came to the barrel, it was full of butter. The old woman was no innocent visitor; she had stolen the cream and strength of the land on that May morning. When she dropped the rope, the power remained in the rope, and the cream of the land filled up the barrel. This story shows how sometimes the harvest and the reward of work could be stolen at the precarious threshold of May morning.

PRESENCE AS SOUL TEXTURE

In the modern workplace, a negative atmosphere can be very destructive. When we speak of an individual, we speak of his presence. Presence is the way a person's individuality comes toward you. Presence is the soul texture of the person. When we speak of this presence in relation to a group of people, we refer to it as atmosphere or ethos. The ethos of a workplace is a very subtle group presence. It is difficult to describe or analyze an ethos; yet you immediately sense its power and effect. Where the ethos is positive, wonderful things can happen. It is a joy to come to work because the atmosphere comes out to meet you, and it is caring, kind, and creative. If the ethos of the workplace is negative and destructive, then when people wake up in the morning, their first thought of going to work literally makes them ill. It is lonely that so many people have to spend so much of their short time in the world in a negative and destructive work ethos. The workplace can be quite hostile; it is often an environment of power. You are working for people who have power over you. They have the power to sack you, criticize and bully you, or compromise your dignity. This is not a welcoming atmosphere. People have power over us because we give our power away to them.

It is an interesting exercise to ask yourself what image you have of the people who have power over you. A friend of mine works in a school that has an insecure principal. He is weak and defensive and uses his power in a very negative way. Recently at a meeting, to start the school term, he berated the staff. The next day my friend ran into this man in town with his wife. She was shocked to recognize that outside of his power context, he looked totally insignificant. This startled her because she had projected such power onto him as school principal.

Sometimes we allow people to exercise destructive power

over us simply because we never question them. When falsity masquerades as power, there is no force that can unmask it as swiftly as a question. We are all familiar with the story of the emperor's new clothes. The emperor paraded through town in what he thought was his new suit, though in reality he was stark naked. Everyone cheered and said what a wonderful suit the emperor wore. They were all in complicit agreement until a little child blurted out the truth. The word of truth is completely powerful. The New Testament says, "Live in the truth and the truth shall set you free." This maxim is relevant to every situation. Gentle, nonconfrontational questions that pursue the truth, as you see it, can prevent a person from taking over all the power in a situation. This will save complex and gentle people from being reduced to the function of an external controlled role.

WEAKNESS AND POWER

Frequently people in power are not as strong as they might wish to appear. Many people who desperately hunger for power are weak. They seek power positions to compensate for their own fragility and vulnerability. A weak person in power can never be generous with power because they see questions or alternative possibilities as threatening their own supremacy and dominance. If you are going to be creatively confrontational with such a person, you need to approach that person very gently in a nondirect manner. This is the only way that the word of your truth can reach such a frightened, powerful person.

The workplace as a place of power can also be a place of control. Control is destructive because it reduces your own independence and autonomy. You are placed back in an infantile role where you are dealing with an authority figure. Because of our untransfigured relationship to our parents, we sometimes turn authority figures into giants. There is a crucial distinction here between power and authority. When you are awake to the integrity of your inner power, then you are your own authority. The word *authority* signifies your authorship of your ideas and actions. The world functions through power structures. Consequently, it is desirable that genuine people of refined sensibility, imagination, and compassion leave themselves available to take up positions of power. A charismatic person in a powerful position can be an agent of far-reaching and positive change.

When you are being controlled, you are treated as an object rather than as a subject. Often people in power have an uncanny instinct at working the system against you. I know a millionaire who made his money in the clothes trade. The women working for him were poorly paid. Every so often, he would sense the tension building up among them. One day he turned the radio on really loud. Then all the workers began to complain. He watched the aggression building up until finally a group came to him and asked that the volume be lowered. He refused. They became more militant and threatened to go on strike. He insisted on keeping the volume loud. When they were almost out on the street, he lowered the volume. His strategy was to let them have the impression that they had the power. Then they returned to work, feeling they had won a victory over the boss, even though he had staged the conflict from the very beginning. This happened forty years ago. In the modern workplace, unionization and the development of workers' rights means that employers can no longer get away with such obvious manipulation. Still the work situation continues to exploit people. Management is now more subtle in its strategies of control and alienation.

The workplace can be a place of great competition. Management sometimes plays workers against each other. Consequently, when you go into work you are in solo combat with your colleague in terms of productivity. Your colleagues begin to appear as a threat. Where productivity becomes God, each individual is reduced to a function. It would be wonderful if the workplace were a place of real inspiration, with the work engaging your creativity. Your gift would be welcomed there; your contribution seen. Everyone has a special gift. Your life becomes happier when your gift can grow and come to expression in your place of work. You are freed to receive inspiration from others. Furthermore, because the gift of each person in relation to the overall work is unique, there need be no competition among the workers. This makes the workplace hospitable to the energies, rhythms, and gifts of the soul. There is no reason why every workplace could not begin to develop such creativity.

Work should not serve the owners and the employers alone. Work should also serve the workers and the community. Structures should be developed whereby workers are able to share in the profits. The entry of imagination and the awakening of soul demand that work be understood as contributing to the creativity and improvement of the larger community. A firm or corporation that has large profits should assist and support the poor and the underprivileged. To create optimal conditions of work should become a priority. Furthermore, awkward but honest questions should be engaged. Work that creates products that endanger people or nature should be critiqued and changed.

One of the most powerful and prophetic analysts of work was Karl Marx. He showed how work can alienate a person from his or her nature and potential. Certain work can dull and darken human presence. In our century, some of the most prophetic, trenchant, and illuminating critical thought has come from this tradition. The school of critical theory has delivered a penetrating evaluation of industrial society. It has revealed that history and society internally influence the structure of human identity. The nature of work and consumerism diminish and oppress the self. Critical theory has made a great contribution to the recovery of soul by identifying the subtlety and pervasiveness of these alienating forces. It cuts through the colorful but fictitious surface image that conceals the quiet suffocation of individuality.

Contemporary society worships at the altar of functionalism. Concepts such as *process, method, model,* and *project* have come to infiltrate our language and determine how we describe our relationship to the world. The recovery of soul means a rediscovery of Otherness; this would awaken again the sense of mystery, possibility, and compassion. The deadening force of function would diminish, and a new vitality would infuse our activities. Stated philosophically, being could find expression in doing. The recovery of the sense of Otherness is the deepest mystical task of modern society. Celtic spirituality has an immense contribution to make in fostering this sense of Otherness. In its metaphysic of friendship, there is a profound acknowledgment of the Otherness of nature, the self, and the divine. However, our modern conversation with Celtic tradition must be critical and reflective; otherwise Celtic spirituality is in danger of becoming another fashionable and exotic spiritual program in our sensate, driven culture.

In the world of negative work, where you are controlled, where power prevails and you are a mere functionary, everything is determined by an ethic of competition. In the world of creative work, where your gift is engaged, there is no competition. The soul transfigures the need for competition. In contrast, the world of quantity is always haunted by competition: If I have less, you have more. But in the world of soul: The more you have, the more everyone has. The rhythm of soul is the surprise of endless enrichment.

THE TRAP OF FALSE BELONGING

This re-imaging of the workplace would help fulfill one of the crucial needs that every individual has: the need to belong. Everyone loves to belong. We want to belong to a group, to a family, and particularly to the place in which we work. Here is the point at which an immense creativity could be released in the workplace. Imagine how lovely it would be if you could be yourself at work and express your true nature, giftedness, and imagination. There need be no separation between your home, your private life, and your actual world of work. One could flow into the other in a creative and mutually enriching way. Instead, too many people belong to the system because they are forced to and controlled.

People are often exceptionally careless in their style of belonging. Too many people belong too naively to the systems in which they are involved. When they are suddenly laid off, or the system collapses, or someone else is promoted, they feel broken, wounded, and demeaned. In nearly every corporation or workplace, you will find many disappointed individuals. Initially, they brought the energy and innocence of their belonging to their work, but they were let down, disappointed, and treated as functionaries. Their energy was claimed and used, but their souls were never engaged.

The heart of the matter: You should never belong fully to something that is outside yourself. It is very important to find a balance in your belonging. You should never belong totally to any cause or system. People frequently need to belong to an external system because they are afraid to belong to their own lives. If your soul is awakened, then you realize that this is the house of your real belonging. Your longing is safe there. *Belonging* is related to *longing*. If you hyphenate *belonging*, it yields a lovely axiom for spiritual growth: Be-Your-Longing. Longing is a precious instinct in the soul. Where you belong should always be worthy of your dignity. You should belong first in your own interiority. If you belong there, and if you are in rhythm with yourself and connected to that deep, unique source within, then you will never be vulnerable when your outside belonging is qualified, relativized, or taken away. You will still be able to stand on your own ground, the ground of your soul, where you are not a tenant, where you are at home. Your interiority is the ground from which nobody can distance, exclude, or exile you. This is your treasure. As the New Testament says, where your treasure is, there is your heart also.

WORK AND IMAGINATION

One of the encouraging aspects of modern work, particularly in the corporate world, is the increasing recognition of the imagination as a vital and essential force. This is not because the corporate world loves the imagination. Corporate appreciation of the imagination has happened for other reasons, namely, the markets are now so volatile and the pace of change so rapid that the old patterns of work control are unproductive. There is a recognition dawning that to have a repetitive linear system controlling the work and the worker is no longer profitable. Consequently, the presence of the soul is now welcome in the workplace. The soul is welcome because it is the place where the imagination lives.

The imagination is the creative force in the individual. It always negotiates different thresholds and releases possibilities of recognition and creativity that the linear, controlling, external mind will never even glimpse. The imagination works on the threshold that runs between light and dark, visible and invisible, quest and question, possibility and fact. The imagination is the great friend of possibility. Where the imagination is awake and alive, fact never hardens or closes but remains open, inviting you to new thresholds of possibility and creativity.

When I was doing my postgraduate work in Germany, I had the good fortune to share a house in Berlin with a wonderful philosopher of science from India who has written some amazing books on the growth of scientific knowledge. Because this man had directed many postgraduate students, I asked him what advice he could give me as I began my research on Hegel. He said that most research tries to establish a conclusion or reach verification that no one can successfully criticize or undermine. Everyone attempts that; there is nothing new in it. I should take a different approach. He said that if I try to discover a few questions in this area that no one has thought of asking, then I will have discovered something truly original and important. This advice was an invitation to novelty, an inspiration to perceive a given situation in a completely new way.

Even though much effort is put into the workplace, the actual application of fresh imagination is rare. Usually a bland sameness is allowed to dominate work. Even the patterns of criticism from workers become predictable and entrenched. Often a new person coming in can bring a new art of questioning and thinking. Suddenly a dead situation coheres itself in a fresh and exciting way. Possibilities that had slept there, under the surface of the old bland similarity, now awaken. People become empowered and engaged; the whole project of that particular workplace comes alive with a new energy. The person who can approach the workplace not with linear analysis, which is so predictable and repetitive, but with imaginative possibility can re-imagine the workplace for its participants and open it up in an engaging and inspiring way. For this reason, the poet, or the artist of soul, has become such an important presence in the contemporary corporate world. An artist can bring a freshness that it severely lacks, opening doors and windows in places that up to then had had impenetrable walls. This approach to the workplace ensures that creativity and spontaneity become major energizing forces there.

SPONTANEITY AND BLOCKAGE

When the workplace is run in a deliberate, forced way, nothing new can happen there. If you try to force the soul, you never succeed. When I was in Germany, my consciousness became intensified and relentlessly active. Consequently, I began to develop a sleep problem. If you are doing physical work during the day, you can survive with very little sleep. If you are doing precise and difficult mental work, you need your sleep. I began to have major insomnia. After rising, I could work for about an hour, then I would be suddenly tired and frustrated. I hated going to bed at night, and every night I made furious attempts to get to sleep. I tried everything. I remember one night being particularly exhausted, and I said to myself, Face it, now you will never sleep properly again. You will never have a night of complete rest. You are going to have this problem for the rest of your life. The strange thing was that as soon as I admitted that to myself, within five minutes I was fast asleep. Over the next few nights my rhythm of sleep returned. What prevented me from sleeping was the deliberate commitment to try to get to sleep. As soon as I let go of the desire to sleep, sleep came naturally.

When the will and the intellect are brought as deliberate forces into the workplace, this only makes the bland similarity even more entrenched. When the imagination, the force of illumination in the soul, is allowed to stir, it opens up the workplace in a completely new way. You should not be neutral or indifferent to your work or workplace. It is very important to have a careful look at the kind of work you do. You should try to establish whether the work you do and your workplace is actually expressive of your identity, dignity, and giftedness. If not, difficult choices may need to be made. If you sell your soul, you ultimately buy a life of misery.

Respectability and security are subtle traps on life's journey. Those who are drawn to extremes are often nearer to renewal and self-discovery. Those trapped in the bland middle region of respectability are lost without ever realizing it. This can be a trap for those addicted to the business world. Many people in business operate only with one side of their mind: the strategic, tactical, mechanical side day in and day out. This becomes a mental habit that they then apply to everything, including their inner life. Even though they may be powerful people in the theater of work, outside of the workplace they look forlorn and lost. You cannot repress the presence of your soul and not pay the price. If you sin against your soul, it is always at great cost. Work can be an attractive way of sinning deeply against the wildness and creativity of your own soul. Work comes to dominate your identity. One of the most disturbing stories in twentieth-century literature portrays the surrealistic destiny of an utterly meticulous and faithful functionary. This is Kafka's *Metamorphosis*, which has the uncanny opening sentence, "As Gregor Samsa awoke one morning out of troubled dreams, he found himself transformed in his bed into a gigantic insect." With deft anonymity, surrealistic detail, and black humor, Kafka is unequaled in his ability to portray systems and their functionaries.

THE ROLE CAN SMOTHER

If you only awaken your will and intellect, then your work can become your identity. This is summed up in the rather humorous epitaph on a gravestone somewhere in London: "Here lies Jeremy Brown born a man and died a grocer." Often people's identities, that wild inner complexity of soul and color of spirit, become shrunken into their work identities. They become prisoners of their roles. They limit and reduce their lives. They become seduced by the practice of self-absence. They move further and further away from their own lives. They are forced backward into hidden areas on the ledges of their hearts. When you encounter them, you meet only the role. You look for the person, but you never meet him. To practice only the linear external side of your mind is very dangerous. Thus the corporate and work world now recognizes how desperately they need the turbulence, anarchy, and growth possibilities that come from the unpredictable world of the imagination. These are so vital for the passion and force of a person's life. If you engage only the external side of yourself, and stay on this mechanical surface, you become secretly weary. Gradually, years of this practice make you desperate.

SISYPHUS

When weariness becomes gravity, it destroys your natural soul protection. It is reminiscent of the myth of Sisyphus, who was condemned for his sin. In the underworld, his task was to roll a huge boulder up a hill. He would painstakingly roll the boulder slowly up and up almost to the summit, then the rock would roll out of his grasp and crash right to the bottom. If Sisyphus could stop and decide never to roll the stone again, he would have peace. But he is the prisoner of the futile and is condemned eternally to begin the same task but never complete it. He has to roll the boulder up the hill eternally in the sure knowledge that he can never get it over the summit. Anyone in the business or corporate work world who remains on the surface of the role, and practices only the linear side of the mind, is like Sisyphus. They are in great danger of a breakdown. A breakdown is often a desperate attempt by the soul to break through the weary facade of role politics. There is a profundity to the human soul that the linear surface of the work world cannot accommodate. When you remain in the rut, you become caged behind one window of the mind. You are then not able to turn around toward the balcony of the soul and enjoy the different views through the other windows of wonder and possibility.

Rapidity is another force causing massive stress in the workplace. Baudrillard, a French philosopher, speaks of the exponential speed of modern life. Where things are moving too quickly, nothing can stabilize, gather, or grow. There is a lovely story of a man exploring Africa. He was in a desperate hurry on a journey through the jungle. He had three or four Africans helping him carry his equipment. They raced onward for about three days. At the end of the third day, the Africans sat down and would not move. He urged them to get up, telling them of the pressure he was under to reach his destination before a certain date. They refused to move. He could not understand this; after much persuasion, they still refused to move. Finally, he got one of them to admit the reason. This native said, "We have moved too quickly to reach here; now we need to wait to give our spirits a chance to catch up with us." Many people who are secretly weary of work have never given themselves time, or taken time out or away from work, to allow their spirits to catch up. Giving yourself plenty of time is a simple but vital reflective exercise: Leave all agendas behind you. Let the neglected presence of your soul come to meet and engage you again. It can be a lovely reacquaintance with your forgotten mystery.

The Celtic imagination testifies to a different concept and experience of time. The recognition of presence and the celebration of nature were only possible because time was a window on the eternal. Time was never reduced to achievement. Time was time for wonder. This is still one of the charming things about Ireland. People here still have time. In contrast to many areas in the Western world, people here inhabit a more flexible and open time rhythm. The ideology of rapidity and clinical efficiency have not gained a grip here, yet.

THE SALMON OF KNOWLEDGE

Surprisingly, there is often great irony in the way the soul behaves. Sometimes in the work world a person with analytic, linear vision can miss out totally on the harvest and fruits of work. The imagination has a particular rhythm of vision that never sees directly in a linear way. The eye of the imagination follows the rhythm of the circle. If your vision is confined to linear purpose, you can miss out on the secret destiny that a form of activity can bring you. There is a lovely, old Celtic

story about Fionn Mac Cumhaill and the salmon of knowledge. Fionn wanted to become a poet. In Celtic Ireland, to be
a poet was a sacred vocation. The poets summed up in themselves a supernatural power, the power of the druid and the
power of creativity. Poets had special access to mysteries that
were not available to the common masses.

There was a salmon in the river Slane in County Meath.
Whoever caught this salmon and ate it would become the
greatest and most gifted poet in Ireland and would also
receive the gift of second sight. There was a man called Fionn
the Seer who had spent seven years pursuing this salmon.
Young Fionn Mac Cumhaill came to him to learn the craft of
poetry. One day Fionn the Seer came back, having caught the
salmon of knowledge. He started a fire and put the salmon on
a spit. The salmon had to be turned very carefully and could
not be burned or the gift would be ruined. After a while the
fire went low, and the salmon could no longer be cooked
properly. Fionn the Seer had no one to gather more wood for
the fire. Just then his protégé, Fionn, came out of the wood,
and he left him to turn the salmon slowly on the spit. Young
Fionn Mac Cumhaill began to turn the salmon, but he was a
dreamer and he allowed his mind to wander. When he looked,
a blister had appeared on the side of the salmon. He grew very
anxious, knowing that Fionn the Seer would be furious with
him for having ruined the salmon. With his thumb he tried
to press the blister back in. As soon as he did, he burned his

thumb, then put it in his mouth to relieve the pain. There was some of the oil of the salmon on his thumb, and as soon as he tasted the salmon oil, he received the wisdom, the gift of second sight, and the vocation of poet. Old Fionn came back with the wood. As soon as he looked at young Fionn's eyes, he knew what had happened. He sat there disappointed that the destiny he had pursued so deliberately had at the last moment turned away from him to be received by an innocent young man who had never even dreamed of such a gift.

This is a good story to illustrate how the linear mind, despite its sincerity and commitment, can totally miss the gift. The imagination in its loyalty to possibility often takes the curved path rather than the linear way. Such risk and openness inherit the harvest of creativity, beauty, and spirit.

Sometimes a person has difficulty with work, not because the work is unsuited to him, or he to it, but because his image of the work is blurred and defective. Frequently, such a person lacks a focus and has allowed the tender presence of his experience to become divided and split. His sense of his work as expression and imagination has been replaced by an image of work as endurance and entrapment.

THE FALSE IMAGE CAN PARALYZE

Perception is crucial to understanding. How you see, and what you see, determine how you will be. Your perception, or your view of reality, is the lens through which you see things. Your perception determines the way things will behave for you and toward you. We tend to perceive difficulty as disturbance. Ironically, difficulty can be a great friend of creativity. I love the lines from Paul Valery: *"Une difficulté est une lumière / Une difficulté insurmontable est un soleil"*—that is, "A difficulty is a light; an insurmountable difficulty is a sun." This is a completely different way of considering the awkward, the uneven, and the difficult. Deep within us, there is a terrible impulse and drive toward perfection. We want everything flattened into the one shape. We do not like unexpected shapes. One of the essential aspects of beginning to re-imagine the workplace is to awaken the ability to welcome that which is difficult and awkward. Frequently, the actual work itself is fine, rather it is our image of it that makes it appear difficult and awkward.

During a phase of my study in Germany, I became acutely aware of the impossibility of my task. I was working on the *Phenomenology of Spirit*. Anyone who knows Hegel will readily admit that this long text is magical but difficult to penetrate. My sense of the difficulty of the project began to mirror itself in my attitude toward the work. Later I began to paralyze myself, and soon I was not able to work at all. As the Germans so beautifully say of such a blockage, *"Ich stehe mir im Weg"*— that is, "I am standing in my own way." I would go to my desk with great commitment, believing that I was going to break through this barrier, but I could not concentrate. The image that kept haunting my mind was the impossibility of my task. Each day I would try anew, but I was totally blocked.

One day I went for a long walk in the forest near Tübingen. In the forest, it suddenly occurred to me that Hegel was not the problem; rather, it was my image of the task that obstructed me. I came back home immediately, sat down, and quickly jotted on a page the image of my work that I had constructed. I recognized the power that the image had. When this became clear to me, I was able to distance the image from the actual work itself. After a couple of days, the image had faded, and I was back into the rhythm of the work.

Some people have a lot of difficulty at work, even though the work is a genuine expression of their nature, giftedness, and potential. The difficulty is not with the work but rather with their image of the work. The image is not merely a surface; it also becomes a lens through which we behold a thing. We are partly responsible for the construction of our own images and completely responsible for how we use them. To recognize that the image is not the person or the thing is liberating.

THE KING AND THE BEGGAR'S GIFT

A difficult or unwanted thing can turn out to be a great gift. Frequently we receive unknown gifts in disguise. There is a wonderful old story told of a young king who took over a kingdom. He was loved before he became a king, and his subjects were delighted when he was finally crowned. They brought him many different gifts. After the coronation, the new king was at supper in the palace. Suddenly, there was a knock at the door. The servants went out to discover an old man shabbily dressed, looking like a beggar. He wanted to see the king. The servants did their best to dissuade him, but to no avail. The king came out to meet him. The old man praised the king, saying how wonderful he was and how delighted everyone in the kingdom was to have him as king. He had brought the king the gift of a melon. The king hated melons. But being kind to the old man, he took the melon, thanked him, and the old man went away happy. The king went indoors and gave the melon to his servants to throw out in the back garden.

The next week at the same time, there was another knock at the door. The king was summoned again and the old man praised the king and offered him another melon. The king took the melon and said good-bye to the old man. Once again, he threw the melon out the back door. This continued for several weeks. The king was too kind to confront the old man or belittle the generosity of the gift that he brought.

Then, one evening, just as the old man was about to hand the melon to the king, a monkey jumped down from a portico in the palace and knocked the melon from the old man's hand. The melon shattered in pieces all over the front of the palace. When the king looked, he saw a shower of diamonds flying from the heart of the melon. Eagerly, he checked the garden at the back of the palace. There, all the melons had melted around a little hillock of jewels. The moral of this story is that sometimes awkward situations, problems, or difficulties are really disguised opportunities for growth. Very often at the heart of the difficulty, there is the light of a great jewel. It is wise to learn to embrace with hospitality that which is awkward and difficult.

My father was an accomplished stonemason. I often watched him building walls. Frequently, he would choose a stone that was completely round. A round stone is useless because it cannot be bound into the structure of the wall. Yet with a little tip of the hammer, my father could transform the stone. Something that looked unformed and awkward would fit into the wall as if it had been made specially for it. I love, too, that image of Michelangelo finding in every stone, no matter how dumb, awkward, or blunt, a secret shape waiting to emerge. Michelangelo's wonderful *Prisoners in Stone* illustrates this. The human figures have almost emerged from the stone, yet from the waist down, they are still trapped in the dull unformed stone. It is an incredible image of arrested release. Very often in difficult work projects, there is a secret shape waiting to emerge. If you concentrate on releasing the hidden possibility within your project, you will find a satisfaction that will surprise you. Meister Eckhart speaks beautifully about the way one should be toward what one does. If you work with a creative and kind eye, you will bring forth beauty.

HEARTFUL WORK BRINGS BEAUTY

When you consider it, the world of your action and activity is a very precious world. What you do should be worthy of you; it should be worthy of your attention and dignity, and conform to your respect for yourself. If you can love what you do, then you will do it beautifully. You might not love your work at the beginning; yet the deeper side of your soul can help you bring the light of love to what you do. Then, regardless of what you do, you will do it in a creative and transforming way.

There is an apposite story about a Zen monk in Japan. The emperor had an absolutely magnificent vase that was ancient and intricately beautiful. One day someone let the vase fall, and it split into millions of fragments. The fragments were gathered up, and the best potter in the land was called to reassemble the vase. He came but failed. He paid for his failure by losing his head. The emperor ordered the next-best potter, and he also failed. This continued for weeks until, finally, all the best artists in the land had died, having failed to reassemble the broken, beautiful vase. There was only one artist left, an old Zen monk who lived in a cave in the mountains. He had a young apprentice. The monk came and collected all the fragments himself and brought them back to his work shed. For weeks and weeks he worked until finally the vase was there again. The apprentice looked at it and thought how beautiful it was. The two of them made the journey to the city and brought the vase into the palace. The emperor and all his courtesans beamed in admiration at the beauty of the reassembled vase. The old Zen monk was graciously rewarded. He and his young apprentice went back to their cave in the mountains. Then, one day, the young apprentice was looking for something and unexpectedly came upon the fragments of the vase. He ran in to his master: "Look at all the fragments of the vase, you never assembled them all. How did you make a vase as beautiful as the ancient one that was broken?" The old master said, "If you do the work that you do from a loving heart, then you will always be able to make something beautiful."

A Blessing

May the light of your soul guide you.

May the light of your soul bless the work you do with the secret love and warmth of your heart.

May you see in what you do the beauty of your own soul.

May the sacredness of your work bring healing, light, and renewal to those who work with you and to those who see and receive your work.

May your work never weary you.

May it release within you wellsprings of refreshment, inspiration, and excitement.

May you be present in what you do.

May you never become lost in the bland absences.
May the day never burden.
May dawn find you awake and alert, approaching your
  new day with dreams, possibilities, and promises.
May evening find you gracious and fulfilled.
May you go into the night blessed, sheltered, and protected.
May your soul calm, console, and renew you.

FIVE

AGING: THE BEAUTY OF THE INNER HARVEST

TIME AS A CIRCLE

The human eye adores gazing; it feasts on the wild beauty of new landscapes, the dignity of trees, the tenderness of a human face, or the white sphere of the moon blessing the earth in a circle of light. The eye is always drawn to the shape of a thing. It finds some deep consolation and sense of home in special shapes. Deep within the human mind, there is a fascination with the circle because it satisfies some longing within us. It is one of the most universal and ancient shapes in the universe. Reality often seems to express itself in this form. The earth is a circle; and even time itself seems to have a circular nature. The Celtic world was always fascinated with circles; they are prevalent in so much of its artwork. The Celts even transfigured the cross by surrounding it with a circle. The Celtic cross is a beautiful symbol. The circle around the beams of the cross rescues the loneliness where the two lines of pain intersect and seems to calm and console their forsaken linearity.

For the Celtic people the world of nature had different domains. First, there was the underworld of nature below the surface of landscape. Here the Tuatha Dé Danann—the fairy people, or the good people—lived. The human world was the middle kingdom between the underworld and the heavenly world. There was no closed or sealed frontier between each of these three worlds. Above, there was the supersensual, or upper, world of the heavens. Each of these three dimensions flowed in and out of each other. Indeed, they participated in each other. It is no wonder, then, that time could be understood as an inclusive and all-embracing circle.

The year is a circle. There is the winter season, which gives away to the spring; then summer grows out of spring until, finally, the year completes itself in the autumn. The circle of time is never broken. This rhythm is even mirrored in the day; it, too, is a circle. First, the new dawn comes out of the darkness, strengthening toward noon, falling away toward evening until night returns again. Because we live in time, the life of each person is also a circle. We come out of the unknown. We appear on the earth, live here, feed off the earth, and eventually return back into the unknown again. The oceans move in this rhythm, too; the tide comes in, turns, and goes back out again. It resembles the rhythm of human breath, which comes in, fills, and then recedes and goes back out again.

The circle brings perspective to the process of aging. As you age, time affects your body, your experience, and above all your soul. There is a great poignancy in aging. When your body ages, you begin to lose the natural and spontaneous vigor of your youthfulness. Time, like a bleak tide, begins to indent the membrane of your strength. It will continue doing that until gradually it empties your life completely. This is one of the most vital questions that affects every person. Can we transfigure the damage that time does to us? Let us pursue this question by first exploring our kinship with nature. Because we are formed from clay, the rhythm of the seasons outside in nature is also active within our own hearts. We can learn much, therefore, from the people who constructed and articulated their spirituality in sisterhood with nature, namely, the Celtic people. They experienced the year as a circle of seasons. Though the Celts had no explicit psychology, they had implicit intuition and great wisdom about the deeper rhythms of human belonging, vulnerability, growth, and diminishment.

THE SEASONS IN THE HEART

There are four seasons within the clay heart. When it is winter in the world of nature, all the colors have vanished; everything is reduced to gray, black, or white. All the visions and beautiful rich coloring of nature thin out completely. Grass disappears from the land, and the earth itself is frozen and perished in a bleak self-retraction. In wintertime, nature withdraws. A tree loses all its leaves and retires inward. When it is wintertime in your life, you are going through pain, difficulty, or turbulence. At such times it is wise to follow the instinct of nature and withdraw into yourself. When it is winter in your soul, it is unwise to pursue any new endeavors. You have to lie low and shelter until this bleak, emptying time passes on. This is nature's remedy. It minds itself in hibernation. When there is great pain in your life, you, too, need sanctuary in the shelter of your own soul.

One of the beautiful transitions in nature is the transition from winter to springtime. An old Zen mystic said that when one flower blooms it is spring everywhere. When the first innocent, infantlike flower appears on the earth, one senses nature stirring beneath the frozen surface. There is a lovely phrase in Gaelic, *ag borradh,* that means there is a quivering life about to break forth. The wonderful colors and the new life the earth receives make spring a time of great exuberance and hope. In a certain sense, spring is the youngest season. Winter is the oldest season. Winter was there from the very beginning. It reigned amidst the silence and bleakness of nature for hundreds of millions of years before vegetation. Spring is a youthful season; it comes forth in a rush of life and promise, hope and possibility. At the heart of the spring, there is a great inner longing. It is the time when desire and memory stir toward each other. Consequently, springtime in your soul is a wonderful time to undertake some new adventure, some new project, or to make some important changes in your life. If you undertake this when it is springtime in your soul, then the rhythm, the energy, and the hidden light of your own clay works with you. You are in the flow of your own growth and potential. Springtime in the soul can be beautiful, hopeful, and strengthening. You can make difficult transitions very naturally in an unforced and spontaneous way.

Spring blossoms and grows into summertime. In summertime, nature is bedecked with color. There is great lushness everywhere, a richness and depth of texture. Summertime is a time of light, growth, and arrival. You feel that the secret life of the year, hidden in the winter and coming out in the spring, has really blossomed in the summertime. Thus summertime in your soul is a time of great balance. You are in the flow of your own nature. You can take as many risks as you like, and you will always land on your feet. There is enough shelter and depth of texture around you to completely ground, balance, and mind you.

Summertime grows into autumn, which is one of my favorite times of the year; seeds sown in the spring and nurtured by the summer now yield their fruit in autumn. It is harvest, the homecoming of the seeds' long and lonely journey through darkness and silence under the earth's surface. Harvest is one of the great feasts of the year. It was a very important time in Celtic culture. The fertility of the earth yielded its fruitfulness. Correspondingly, when it is autumn in your life, the things that happened in the past, or the experiences that were sown in the clay of your heart, almost unknown to you, now yield their fruit. Autumntime in a person's life can be a time of great gathering. It is a time for harvesting the fruits of your experiences.

AUTUMN AND THE INNER HARVEST

These are the four seasons of the heart. Several seasons can be present simultaneously in the heart, though usually, at any one time, one season is dominant in your life. It is customary to understand autumn as synchronous with old age. In the autumntime of your life, your experience is harvested. This is a lovely backdrop against which we can understand aging. Aging is not merely about the body losing its poise, strength, and self-trust. Aging also invites you to become aware of the sacred circle that shelters your life. Within the harvest circle, you are able to gather lost moments and experiences, bring them together, and hold them as one. In actual fact, if you can come to see aging not as the demise of your body but as the harvest of your soul, you will learn that aging can be a time of great strength, poise, and confidence. To understand the harvest of your soul against the background of seasonal rhythm should give you a sense of quiet delight at the arrival of this time in your life. It should give you strength and a sense of how the deeper belonging of your soul-world will be revealed to you.

Even though the body ages, diminishes, becomes frail, weak, and ill, the shelter of the soul around the body always embraces that fragility tenderly. That the body is in the soul is a great consolation and shelter. As your body ages, you can become aware of how your soul enfolds and minds your body; and the panic and fear often associated with aging can fall away from you. This can bring you a deeper sense of strength, belonging, and poise. Aging is so frightening because it seems that your autonomy and independence are forsaking you against your will. To the young, old people seem ancient. When you begin to age yourself, you recognize how incredibly quickly time is moving. But the only difference between a young person at the height of their exuberance and a very old person who is frail and physically wasted is time.

One of the greatest mysteries in life is the mystery of time. Everything that happens to us, happens to us in and through time. Time is the force that brings every new experience to the door of your heart. All that happens to you is controlled and determined by time. The poet Paul Murray speaks of the moment as "the place of pilgrimage to which I am a pilgrim."

Time opens up and opens out the mystery of the soul. The transience and the mysteries that time unfolds have always filled me with reverence and wonder. This found expression in one of my poems, called "Cottage":

> I sit alert
> behind the small window
> of my mind and watch
> the days pass, strangers
> who have no reason to look in.

Time in this sense can be very frightening. All around the human body is nothingness; that nothingness is the air element. There is no obvious, physical protection around your body, therefore anything can approach you at any time, from any direction. The clear empty air will not stop the arrows of destiny from lodging in your life. Life is incredibly contingent and unexpected.

TRANSIENCE MAKES A GHOST OF EXPERIENCE

One of the loneliest aspects of time is transience. Time passes and takes everything away. This can be consoling when you are suffering and going through a lonely, searing time. It is encouraging to be able to say to yourself, This, too, will pass. But the opposite is also true when you are having a lovely time and are really happy; you are with the person you love, and life could not be better. On such a perfect evening or day, you secretly say to your heart, God I wish this could continue forever. But it cannot; this, too, comes to an end. Even Faust begged the moment to stay: *"Verweile doch, Du bist so schon"*— that is, "Linger awhile, for you are so beautiful."

Transience is the force of time that makes a ghost of every experience. There was never a dawn, regardless how beautiful or promising, that did not grow into noontime. There was never a noon that did not fall into afternoon. There was never an afternoon that did not fade toward evening. There never was a day yet that did not get buried in the graveyard of the night. In this way transience makes a ghost out of everything that happens to us.

All of our time disappears on us. This is an incredible fact. You are so knitted into a day. You are within it; the day is as close as your skin. It is around your eyes; it is inside your mind. The day moves you, often it can weigh you down; or again it can raise you up. Yet the amazing fact is, this day vanishes. When you look behind you, you do not see your past standing there in a series of day shapes. You cannot wander back through the gallery of your past. Your days have disappeared silently and forever. Your future time has not arrived yet. The only ground of time is the present moment.

In our culture, we place a great and worthy emphasis on the importance and sacredness of experience. In other words, what you think, believe, or feel remains a fantasy if it does not actually become part of the fabric of your experience. Experience is the touchstone of verification, credibility, and deep intimacy. Yet the future of every experience is its disappearance. This raises a fascinating question: Is there a place where our vanished days secretly gather? As a medieval mystic asked, Where does the light go when the candle is blown out? I believe that there is a place where our vanished days secretly gather. The name of that place is memory.

MEMORY: WHERE OUR VANISHED DAYS SECRETLY GATHER

Memory is one of the most beautiful realities of the soul. Since the body itself is so linked into the visual sense it often does not recognize memory as the place where the past is gathered. The most powerful image of memory is the tree. I remember seeing once at the Museum of Natural History in London a sliver of the diameter of a giant redwood from California. This tree's memory reached back to about the fifth century. The memory rings within the diameter of the tree had little white flags at different points documenting the age of the particular memory ring. The first one was St. Colmcille going to Iona in the sixth century, then up along the Renaissance, the seventeenth and eighteenth centuries on up to the twentieth century. This giant redwood had lived through fourteen or fifteen centuries of time. Its great memory had unfolded all that time within the texture of its timber.

In the classical tradition, the most beautiful evocation of the power, presence, and riches of memory is in book 10 of St. Augustine's confession. The following passage is splendid in its portrayal of the inner world.

> Great is the power of memory, exceedingly great, O my God, a spreading limitless room within me. Who can reach its uttermost depth? Yet it is a faculty of soul and belongs to my nature. In fact I cannot totally grasp all that I am. Thus the mind is not large enough to contain itself but where can the part of it be which it does not contain? Is it outside itself and not within? As this question struck I was overcome with wonder and almost stupor. Here are men going afar to marvel at the heights of the mountains, the mighty waves of the sea, the long courses of great rivers, the vastness of the ocean, the movement of the stars, yet leaving themselves, unnoticed and not seeing it as marvelous that when I spoke of all these things, I did not see them with my eyes, yet I could not have spoken of them unless these mountains and waves and rivers and stars which I have seen, and the ocean of which I have heard, had been inwardly present to my sight: in my memory, yet with the same vast spaces between them as if I saw them outside me.

One of the great poverties of our modern culture of rapidity, stress, and externality is that there is so little attention to memory. The computer industry has hijacked the notion of memory. To say that computers have memory is false. A computer has storage and recall. Human memory is, however, more refined, sacred, and personal. Memory has its own inner selectivity and depth. Human memory is an inner temple of feeling and sensibility. Within that temple different experiences are grouped according to their particular feeling and shape. Our time suffers from a great amnesia. The American philosopher Santayana said, "Those who cannot remember the past are condemned to repeat it."

The beauty and invitation of old age offer a time of silence and solitude for a visit to the house of your inner memory. You can revisit all of your past. Your soul is the place where your memory lives. Since linear time vanishes, everything depends on memory. In other words, our time comes in yesterdays, todays, and tomorrows. Yet there is another place within us that lives in eternal time. That place is called the soul. The soul, therefore, lives mainly in the mode of eternity. This means that as things happen in your yesterdays, todays, and tomorrows and fall away with transience, they fall and are caught and held by the net of the eternal in your soul. There they are gathered, preserved, and minded for you. Levinas says, "Memory as an inversion of historical time is the essence of interiority." Consequently, as your body ages and gets weaker, your soul is in fact getting richer, deeper, and stronger. With time your soul grows more sure of itself; the natural light within it increases and brightens. There is a beautiful poem by the wonderful Czeslaw Milosz on old age called "A New Province." This is the last verse:

> I would prefer to be able to say: "I am satiated,
> What is given to taste in this life, I have tasted."
> But I am like someone in a window who draws aside a
>   curtain
> To look at a feast he does not comprehend.

TÍR NA N-ÓG: THE LAND OF YOUTH

The Celtic tradition had a wonderful sense of the way eternal time is woven through our human time. There is the lovely story of Oisín, who was one of the Fianna, a band of Celtic warriors. He was tempted to visit the land called Tír na n-Óg, which is the land of eternal youth, where the good people, the fairy people, lived. Oisín went off with them, and for a long, long time he lived happily there with his woman, Niamh Cinn Oir, known as Niamh of the golden hair. The time seemed so short to him, being a time of great joy. The quality of our experience always determines the actual rhythm of time. When you are in pain, every moment slows down until it resembles a week. When you are happy and really enjoying your life, time flies. Oisin's time passed really quickly in the land of Tír na n-Óg. Then his longing for his old life began to gnaw. He began to wonder how the Fianna were, and what was happening in Ireland. He began to long for home, the land of Éire. The fairy people discouraged him because they knew that as a former inhabitant of mortal and linear time, he would be in danger of getting lost there forever. Nevertheless, he decided to return. They gave him a beautiful white horse and told him never to dismount. If he did, he would be lost. He came on the great white horse back to the land of Ireland. Greater loneliness awaited him when he discovered that he had been gone for hundreds and hundreds of years. The Fianna had disappeared. He consoled himself by visiting their old hunting sites and the places where they had feasted, sung, recited old stories, and achieved great feats of valor. In the meantime, Christianity had come to Ireland. When Oisín was riding around on his white horse, he saw a group of men failing as they attempted to raise a big rock to build a church. Being a warrior, he had wonderful strength, and he looked at them and longed to help them; but he knew he dare not dismount from the horse; if he did, he was lost. He watched them from a distance for a while, then he rode nearer. He could not resist any longer. He took his foot out of the stirrup and reached under the rock to raise it up for them, but as soon as he did, the girth broke, the saddle turned over, and Oisín hit the ground. The very moment he hit the land of Ireland, he became a feeble, wrinkled old man. This is a wonderful story to show the coexistence of the two levels of time. If you broke the threshold that the fairies observed between these two levels of time, you ended up stranded in mortal, linear time. The destination of human time is death. Eternal time is unbroken presence.

ETERNAL TIME

This story also shows that there is a different rhythm of life in eternal time. One night, a man from our village was coming back home along a road where there were no houses. Cycling along, he heard beautiful music. The music was coming from inside the wall by the sea. He crossed over the wall to find that he was entering a village in this forsaken place. The people there seemed to have expected him. They seemed to know him; and he received a great welcome. He was given drink and delicious food. Their music was more beautiful than he had ever heard before. He spent a few hours of great happiness there. Then he remembered that if he did not return home, they would be out searching for him. He bade farewell to the villagers. When he arrived home, he discovered that he had been missing for a fortnight even though it had seemed like half an hour in the eternal, fairy world.

My father used to tell another such story about a monk

named Phoenix, who one day in the monastery was reading his breviary. A bird began to sing, and the monk listened so purely to the song of the bird that he was aware of nothing else. Then the song stopped, and he took up his breviary and went back into the monastery to discover that he no longer recognized anyone there. And they did not recognize him either. He named all his fellow monks with whom he had lived up to what seemed half an hour before, but they had all disappeared. The new monks looked up their annals, and sure enough, years and years before, a monk Phoenix had mysteriously disappeared. At the metaphorical level, this story claims that through real presence the monk Phoenix had actually broken into eternal time. Eternal time moves in a different rhythm from normal, broken human time. Oscar Wilde said, "We think in eternity but we move slowly through time." This beautiful phrase echoes powerfully because it comes from "De Profundis," Wilde's letter of love and forgiveness to one who betrayed and destroyed him.

These Celtic fairy stories suggest a region of the soul that inhabits the eternal. There is an eternal region within us where we are not vulnerable to the ravages of normal time. Shakespeare expressed the ravages of calendar time beautifully in Sonnet 60:

Like as the waves make towards the pebbled shore,
so do our minutes hasten to their end

each changing place with that which goes before
in sequent toil all forwards do contend.

THE SOUL AS TEMPLE OF MEMORY

The Celtic stories suggest that time as the rhythm of soul has an eternal dimension where everything is gathered and minded. Here nothing is lost. This is a great consolation: The happenings in your life do not disappear. Nothing is ever lost or forgotten. Everything is stored within your soul in the temple of memory. Therefore, as an old person, you can happily go back and attend to your past time; you can return through the rooms of that temple, visit the days that you enjoyed and the times of difficulty where you grew and refined yourself. Old age, as the harvest of life, is a time when your times and their fragments gather. In this way, you unify yourself and achieve a new strength, poise, and belonging that was never available to you when you were distractedly rushing through your days. Old age is a time of coming home to your deeper nature, of entering fully into the temple of your memory where all your vanished days are secretly gathered and awaiting you.

The idea of memory was very important in Celtic spirituality. There are lovely prayers for different occasions. There are prayers for the hearth, for kindling the fire, and for smooring the hearth. At night, the ashes were smoored over the burning coals, sealing off the air. The next morning the coals would still be alive and burning. There is also a lovely prayer for the hearth keepers that evokes St. Bridget, who was both a pagan Celtic goddess and a Christian saint. In herself, Bridget focuses the two worlds easily and naturally. The pagan world and the Christian world have no row with each other in the Irish psyche, rather they come close to each other in a lovely way. This is a nice prayer for the hearth that also recognizes memory:

Brighid of the mantle encompass us,
Lady of the Lambs protect us,
Keeper of the Hearth, kindle us,
Beneath your mantle, gather us
And restore us to memory

Mothers of our mother,
Foremothers strong,
Guide our hands in yours
Remind us how
To kindle the hearth,

To keep it bright
To preserve the flame,
Your hands upon ours,
Our hands within yours,

To kindle the light,
Both day and night

The mantle of Brighid about us,
The memory of Brighid within us,
The protection of Brighid keeping us
From harm, from ignorance, from heartlessness,
This day and night,
From dawn till dark
From dark to dawn.

(COMP. CAITLÍN MATTHEWS)

This is a fine recognition of the circle of memory holding everything together in a hospitable unity.

In a positive sense, aging becomes a time for visiting the temple of your memory and integrating your life. Integration is a vital part of coming home to yourself. What is not integrated remains fragmented; sometimes it can come to great conflict within you. The presence and process of integration brings you more fully home to yourself. There is so much that needs to be integrated within each person. Camus said aptly that after one day in the world you could spend the rest of your life in solitary confinement and you would still have dimensions of that day's experience left to decipher. So much happens to us of which we are unaware even within the simple circle of a day. To visit the temple of memory is not merely to journey back to the past; it is rather to awaken and integrate everything that happens to you. It is part of the process of reflection that gives depth to experience. We all have experiences, but as T. S. Eliot said, we had the experience but missed the meaning. Every human heart seeks meaning; for it is in meaning that our deepest shelter lies. Meaning is the sister of experience, and to discern the meaning of what has happened to you is one of the essential ways of finding your inner belonging and discovering the sheltering presence of your soul. There is an amazing line in the Bible from the prophet Haggai: "You have sown so much but harvested so little." Everything that happens to you is an act of sowing a seed of experience. It is equally important to be able to harvest that experience.

SELF-COMPASSION AND THE ART OF INNER HARVESTING

Old age can be a wonderful time to develop the art of inner harvesting. What does inner harvesting mean? Inner harvesting means that you actually begin to sift the fruits of your experience. You begin to group, select, and integrate them. One of the places where inner harvesting is most vital is in the abandoned areas within your life. Areas of inner neglect and abandonment cry out to you. They are urgent for harvest. Then they can come in out of the false exile of neglect and enter into the temple of belonging, the soul. This is particularly necessary in relation to the things that you have found difficult in your life, things to which you had great resistance. Above all, your inner wounds cry out for healing. There are two ways of doing this. You can do it in an analysis-driven way, where you go back to the wound and open it up again. You take off the protective healing skin that has grown around it. You make it sore, and you make it weep again. A lot of therapy reverses the process of healing. Maybe there is a less intrusive art of attention that you can bring to your wounds. For the soul has its own natural rhythm of healing. Consequently, many of your wounds are very well healed and should not be opened up again. If you want to, you could select a list of your wounds and spend the next thirty years opening them up until eventually you become like Job with your body a mass of sores. If you engage in this practice of woundology, you will turn your soul into a mass of weeping sores. Each of us has a wonderful but precarious freedom in relation to our inner life. We need, therefore, to treat ourselves with great tenderness.

Part of the wisdom of spiritual soulful self-presence is to be able to let certain aspects of your life alone. This is the art of spiritual noninterference. Yet other aspects of your life call urgently for your attention; they call to you as their shelterer to come and harvest them. You can discern where these wounds are in the temple of memory, then visit them in a gentle and mindful way. The one kind of creative presence you could bring to these areas is compassion. Some people can be very compassionate to others but are exceptionally harsh with themselves. One of the qualities that you can develop, particularly in your older years, is a sense of great compassion for yourself. When you visit the wounds within the temple of memory, you should not blame yourself for making bad mistakes that you greatly regret. Sometimes you have grown unexpectedly through these mistakes. Frequently, in a journey of the soul, the most precious moments are the mistakes. They have brought you to a place that you would otherwise have always avoided. You should bring a compassionate mindfulness to your mistakes and wounds. Endeavor to inhabit again the rhythm you were in at that time. If you visit this configuration of your soul with forgiveness in your heart, it will fall into place itself. When you forgive yourself, the inner wounds begin to heal. You come in out of the exile of hurt into the joy of inner belonging. This art of integration is very precious. You have to trust your deeper, inner voice to know which places you need to visit. This is not to be viewed in a quantitative way, but rather in a gentle, spiritual way. If you bring that kind light to your soul and to its wounded places, you can effect incredible inner healing.

To Keep Something Beautiful in Your Heart

The soul is the natural shelter around your life. If, during your life, you have not continually scraped away this shelter, your soul will now gather around you to mind you. To approach your soul and memory with neon analysis can be very destructive, especially in the vulnerability of your old age. You should let your soul be natural. From this perspective old age can be a vulnerable time. Many people, as they age, get very worried and anxious. It is precisely when times are difficult and you are vulnerable that you really have to mind yourself. I love Blaise Pascal's idea that in a difficult time, you should always keep something beautiful in your heart. Perhaps, as a poet said, it is beauty that will save us in the end.

How you view your future actually shapes it. In other words, expectation helps create the future. Many of our troubles do not belong to us. They are troubles we draw upon ourselves through our gloomy attitude. There is a friend of mine from Cork who lived near an old woman named Mary who had a notoriously negative and gloomy outlook on everything. She always had the "bad word." A neighbor met her one beautiful May morning. The sun was shining, flowers were out, and nature looked as if it wanted to dance. He said to her, "God, isn't it a beautiful morning, Mary." She replied, "I know sure, but what about tomorrow?" She was not able to enjoy the actual presence of beauty around her because she was already troubled by how awful tomorrow was going to be. Troubles are not just constellations of the soul or consciousness; frequently, they actually assume a spirit form.

Perhaps there are little crowds of miseries flying along through the air. Then they look down and see you gloomy and miserable. They imagine if they come down they might be able to lodge for a week or a few months or even a year. If you let your own natural shelter down, these miseries can come in and take up tenancy in different places in your mind. The longer you leave them there, the harder it will be to evict them in the end. Natural wisdom seems to suggest that the way you are toward your life is the way that your life will be toward you. To have an attitude that is compassionate and hopeful brings home to you the things you really need.

Old age is a time of second innocence. There is the first innocence when we are children; but that innocence is based on naive trust and ignorance. The second innocence comes later in your life, when you have lived deeply. You know the bleakness of life, you know its incredible capacity to disappoint and sometimes destroy. Yet notwithstanding that realistic recognition of life's negative potential, you still maintain an outlook that is wholesome and hopeful and bright. That is a kind of second innocence. It is lovely to meet an old person whose face is deeply lined, a face that has been deeply inhabited, to look in the eyes and find light there. That light is innocent; it is not inexperienced but rather is innocent in its trust in the good and the true and the beautiful. Such a gaze from an old face is a kind of blessing. You feel good and wholesome in that kind of company.

THE BRIGHT FIELD

One of the most destructive negative attitudes toward one's past or toward one's memory is the attitude of regret. Often regret is very false and displaced, and imagines the past to be totally other than it was. Edith Piaf's song *"Je ne regrette rien"* is wonderful in its free and wild acceptance.

I know a wild woman who has lived a very unprotected life. She has had a lot of trouble, and things have often gone wrong for her. I remember that she said to me one time, "I don't regret a bit of it. It is my life, and in everything negative that happened to me, there was always something bright hidden." She brought a lovely integrating perspective to her past, a way to retrieve treasures that were hidden in past difficulties. Sometimes difficulty is the greatest friend of the soul. There is a beautiful poem by the Welsh poet R. S. Thomas about looking back on life feeling, maybe, that you missed something or that you regret something that you did not do. It is called "The Bright Field":

> I have seen the light break through
> to illuminate a small field
> for a while and gone my way
> and forgotten it. But that was the pearl
> of great prize, the one field that had
> the treasure in it. I realize now

that I must give all that I have
to possess it. Life is not hurrying

on to a receding future nor hankering after
an imagined past. It is the turning
aside like Moses to the miracle
of the lit bush. To a brightness
that seems as transitory as your youth
once, but is the eternity that awaits you.

At the heart of R. S. Thomas's beautiful poem is a Celtic idea of time. Your time is not just past or future. Your time here always inhabits the circle of your soul. All your time is gathered, and even your future time is waiting here for you. In a certain sense your past is not gone but rather is hidden in your memory. Your time is the deeper seed of the eternity that is waiting to welcome you.

THE PASSIONATE HEART NEVER AGES

Often old people have a touching mellowness about them. Age is not dependent on chronological time. Age is more related to a person's temperament. I know some young people who are about eighteen or twenty that are so serious, grave, and gloomy that they sound like ninety-year-olds. Conversely, I know some very old people who have hearts full of roguery, devilment, and fun; there is a sparkle in their presence. When you meet them, you have a sense of light, lightness, and gaiety. Sometimes in very old bodies there are incredibly young, wild souls looking out at you. It is so invigorating to meet a wild old person who has remained faithful to their wild life force. Meister Eckhart said that, too, in a more formal way: There is a place in the soul that is eternal. He says time makes you old, but that there is a place in the soul that time cannot touch. It is a lovely thing to know this about yourself. Even though time will inscribe your face, weaken your limbs, make your movements slower, and, finally, empty your life, nevertheless there is still a place in your spirit that time can never get near. You are as young as you feel. If you begin to feel the warmth of your soul, there will be a youthfulness in you that no one will ever be able to take away from you. Put more formally, this is a way of inhabiting the eternal side of your life. It would be sad on your one journey through life to miss out on this eternal presence around you and within you.

When you are young you have a great intensity and sense of adventure. You want to do everything. You want it all, and you want it now. Your young life is usually not a time for reflection. That is why Goethe said that youth is wasted on the young. You are going in all directions, and you are not sure of your way. A neighbor of mine has a lot of difficulty with alcohol. The nearest pub is in the next town. If he wanted to get a ride to the pub, he would have to go to the next village, which lies in the opposite direction. My brother passed this man on the road one evening. He stopped the car to give him a ride. But he refused, saying, "Even though I'm walking this way I'm going the other way." Many people today are walking one way, but their lives are going in the other direction. Old age offers the opportunity to integrate and bring together the multiplicity of directions that you have traveled. It is a time when you can bring the circle of your life together to where your longing can be awakened and new possibilities can come alive for you.

THE FIRE OF LONGING

Modern society is based on an ideology of strength and image. Consequently, old people are often sidelined. Modern culture is totally obsessed with externality, image, speed, and change; it is driven. In former times, old people were seen as those who had the greatest wisdom. There was always reverence and respect for the elders. Old people still have the fires of longing burning brightly and beautifully within their hearts. Our idea of beauty is impoverished now because beauty is reduced to good looks. There is a whole cult of youthfulness where everyone is trying to look youthful; people have face-lifts and try endless methods to keep the image of youth. But this is not beauty at all. Real beauty is a light that comes from the soul. Sometimes in an old face, you see that light coming from behind the lines; it is a vision of the most poignant beauty.

That passion and longing are beautifully expressed in Yeats's
poem "The Song of Wandering Aengus":

> I went out to the hazel wood,
> Because a fire was in my head,
> And cut and peeled a hazel wand,
> And hooked a berry to a thread.
> And when white moths were on the wing
> And moth-like stars were flickering out,
> I dropped the berry in a stream
> And caught a little silver trout.
>
> When I had laid it on the floor
> I went to blow the fire aflame,
> But something rustled on the floor,
> And some one called me by my name.
> It had become a glimmering girl
> With apple blossom in her hair
> Who called me by my name and ran
> And faded through the brightening air.
>
> Though I am old with wandering
> Through hollow lands and hilly lands,
> I will find out where she has gone,
> And kiss her lips and take her hands;
> And walk among long dappled grass,

And pluck till time and times are done
The silver apples of the moon,
The golden apples of the sun.

AGING: AN INVITATION TO NEW SOLITUDE

The new solitude in your life can make the prospect of aging frightening. A new quietness settles on the outer frame of your active life, on the work that you have done, the family that you have raised, and the role that you have played. Your life takes on a greater stillness and solitude. These facts need not be frightening. If you view them creatively, your new stillness and solitude can be wonderful gifts and great resources for you. Time and again, we miss out on the great treasures in our lives because we are so restless. In our minds we are always elsewhere. We are seldom in the place where we stand and in the time that is now. Many people are haunted by the past, things that they have not done, things that they should have done that they regret not doing. They are prisoners of their past. Other people are haunted by the future; they are anxious and worried about what is coming.

Few people are actually able to inhabit their present time because they are too stressed and rushed. One of the joys of aging is that you have more time to be still. Pascal said that many of our major problems derive from our inability to sit still in a room. Stillness is vital to the world of the soul. If as you age you become more still, you will discover that stillness can be a great companion. The fragments of your life will have time to unify, and the places where your soul-shelter is wounded or broken will have time to knit and heal. You will be able to return to yourself. In this stillness, you will engage your soul. Many people miss out on themselves completely as they journey through life. They know others, they know places, they know skills, they know their work, but tragically, they do not know themselves at all. Aging can be a lovely time of ripening when you actually meet yourself, indeed maybe for the first time. There are beautiful lines from T. S. Eliot that say

> And the end of all our exploring
> Will be to arrive where we started
> And to know the place for the first time.

LONELINESS: THE KEY TO COURAGE

When you are too familiar with who you are, you have become in fact a real stranger to yourself. As you age, you will have more space to become acquainted with yourself. This solitude can take the form of loneliness, and as you age you can become very lonely. Loneliness is exceptionally difficult. A friend who was living in Germany told me of his battle with homesickness. He found the temperament, the order, the structures, and the externality of Germany very difficult. He had the flu during the winter, and the loneliness he had repressed came out to haunt him. He got desperately lonely, but instead of avoiding it, he decided to allow the loneliness to have its way. He sat down in the armchair and gave himself permission to feel as lonely as he wanted. As soon as he gave that invitation to his soul, the loneliness just poured through him. He felt like the most abandoned orphan in the cosmos. He cried and cried. In a way, he was crying for all the loneliness in his life that he had kept hidden. Though this was painful, it was a wonderful experience for him. When he let the loneliness flow, let the dam burst within, something shifted in his relation to his own loneliness. He was never again lonely in Germany. He became free once he had met the depth of his own loneliness, engaged and befriended it. It became a natural part of his life. An old friend of mine in Connemara said one evening as we were talking about loneliness, *"Is poll dubh dóite é an t-uaigness, ach má dhúnann tú suas é, dúnfaidh tú amach go leor eile atá go h-álainn chomh maith"*—that is, "Loneliness is a black burnt hole, but if you close it up, you close out so much that can be so beautiful for you as well." There is no need for us to be afraid of that loneliness. If we engage it, it can bring us new freedom.

WISDOM AS POISE AND GRACE

Wisdom is another quality of old age. In former societies, the old people were called elders because it was recognized that having lived so long, they had harvested wisdom. Our culture is absolutely obsessed with information. There is more information now available in the world than ever before. We have so much knowledge about every possible thing. Yet there is great difference between knowledge and wisdom. You can know many things, you can know a lot of facts about things, even facts about yourself, but it is the truths that you realize yourself that move deeply into you. Wisdom, then, is a deeper way of knowing. Wisdom is the art of living in rhythm with your soul, your life, and the divine. Wisdom is the way that you learn to decipher the unknown; and the unknown is our closest companion. So wisdom is the art of being courageous and generous with the unknown, of being able to decipher and recognize its treasures. In Celtic culture, and in the old Irish Celtic world, there was immense respect for wisdom. Since the Celtic world was primarily a matriarchal society, very many of these wise people were women. The Celts had a wonderful tradition of wisdom, which subsequently continued down into Irish monasticism. When Europe was going through the Dark Ages, it was the monks from Ireland who preserved the memory of learning. They set up centers of learning all over Europe. The Irish monks recivilized Europe. That learning became the basis of the wonderful medieval scholasticism and its rich culture.

Traditionally in Ireland each region had its own wise person. In County Clare, there was a wise woman called Biddy Early. In Galway there was a woman called Cailleach an

Clochain or the old woman of Clifden, who also had this wisdom. When people were confused in their lives, or worried
about the future, they would often visit these wise figures.
Through their counsel, people learned to engage their destiny
anew; they learned to live more deeply and enjoy protection
from imminent danger and destruction. Wisdom is often
associated with the harvesttime of life. That which is scat-
tered has no unity, whereas that which is gathered comes
home to unity and belonging. Wisdom, then, is the art of
balancing the known with the unknown, the suffering with
the joy; it is a way of linking the whole of life together in a
new and deeper unity. Our society would be very well advised
to attend to the wisdom of old people, to integrate them into
the processes of decision making. The wisdom of the aged
could be invaluable in helping us to articulate a vision for our
future. Ultimately, wisdom and vision are sisters; the creativity, critique, and prophecy of vision issue from the fount of
wisdom. Older people are great treasure-houses of wisdom.

OLD AGE AND THE TWILIGHT TREASURES

Old age is also the twilight time of life. On the west coast of
Ireland the light is really magical. Many artists come to work
in this light. Twilight in the west of Ireland is a time of beautiful colors. It is as if the latent colors of the day, which were
lost under the whiteness of the light, now have the courage to

emerge; every color has a great depth. The day bids us adieu in such a dignified and beautiful way. The day's farewell is expressed in twilight, in the magic of color and beauty. The twilight makes the night welcome. It is as if the beautiful colors of twilight slip into the night and make the night habitable and bearable, a place where there is hidden light. Similarly, in old age, the twilight time of life, many of the unnoticed treasures in your life can now become available and visible to you. Often it is only with the twilight perception that you can really glimpse the mysteries of your soul. When the neon light of analysis grasps at the soul, the soul rushes to conceal and hide itself. Twilight perception can be a threshold to invite the shy soul to come closer to you in order to glimpse its beautiful lineaments of longing and possibility.

OLD AGE AND FREEDOM

Old age can also be a time of clearance. All perception requires clearance. If things are too close to you, you cannot see them. Frequently that is why we value so little the people who are really close to us. We are unable to step back and behold them with the sense of wonder, critique, and appreciation they deserve. Nor do we behold ourselves either, because we are too close to the rush of our lives. In old age, as your life calms, you will be able to make many clearances in order to see who you are, what life has done to you, and what you have made of your life. Old age can be a time of releasing the many false burdens that you have dragged behind you through stony fields of years. Sometimes the greatest burdens humans carry are the burdens they make for themselves. People who put years into constructing a heavy burden for themselves often say, Sure it is my cross in life, God help me, I hope God will reward me for carrying it. This is nonsense. Looking down and seeing a people carrying burdens they have invented and created themselves, God must think, How foolish they are to think that it has anything to do with my destiny for them. It has more to do with their own negative use of the freedom and possibility that I give them. False burdens can fall away in old age. One possible way to begin would be to ask yourself, What are the lonely burdens that you have carried? Some of them would definitely belong to you, but more of them you have just picked up and made for yourself. To begin to let them go is to lighten the pressure and weight on your life. You will then experience a lightness and a great inner freedom. Freedom can be one of the wonderful fruits of old age. You can undo the damage that you did to yourself early on in your life. This whole complex of possibility is summed up magnificently by the wonderful Mexican poet Octavio Paz:

> With great difficulty advancing by millimetres each year, I carve a road out of the rock. For millenniums my teeth have wasted and my nails broken to get there, to the other side,

to the light and the open air. And now that my hands bleed and my teeth tremble, unsure in a cavity cracked by thirst and dust, I pause and contemplate my work. I have spent the second part of my life breaking the stones, drilling the walls, smashing the doors, removing the obstacles I placed between the light and myself in the first part of my life.

A Blessing for Old Age

May the light of your soul mind you,
May all of your worry and anxiousness about becoming old
* be transfigured,*
May you be given a wisdom with the eye of your soul,
to see this beautiful time of harvesting.
May you have the commitment to harvest your life,
to heal what has hurt you, to allow it to come closer to you
* and become one with you.*
May you have great dignity, may you have a sense of how
* free you are,*
and above all may you be given the wonderful gift of meeting
* the eternal light*
and beauty that is within you.
May you be blessed, and may you find a wonderful love in
* yourself for yourself.*

SIX

DEATH: THE HORIZON IS IN THE WELL

THE UNKNOWN COMPANION

There is a presence who walks the road of life with you. This presence accompanies your every moment. It shadows your every thought and feeling. On your own, or with others, it is always there with you. When you were born, it came out of the womb with you, but with the excitement at your arrival, nobody noticed it. Though this presence surrounds you, you may still be blind to its companionship. The name of this presence is death.

We are wrong to think that death comes only at the end of life. Your physical death is but the completion of a process on which your secret companion has been working since your birth. Your life is the life of your body and soul, but the presence of your death enfolds both. How does death manifest itself to us in our day-to-day experience? Death meets us in and through different guises in the areas of our life where we are vulnerable, frail, hurting, or negative. One of the faces of death is negativity. In every person there is some wound of negativity; this is like a blister on your life. You can be quite destructive toward yourself, even when times are good. Some people are having wonderful lives right now, but they do not actually realize it. Maybe later on, when things become really difficult or desperate, a person will look back on these times and say, "You know, I was really happy then but sadly I never realized it."

THE FACES OF DEATH IN EVERYDAY LIFE

There is a gravity within that continually weighs on us and pulls us away from the light. Negativity is an addiction to the bleak shadow that lingers around every human form. Within a poetics of growth or spiritual life, the transfiguration of this negativity is one of our continuing tasks. This negativity is the force and face of your own death gnawing at your belonging in the world. It wants to make you a stranger in your own life. This negativity holds you outside in exile from your own love and warmth. You can transfigure negativity by turning it toward the light of your soul. This soul-light gradually takes the gravity, weight, and hurt out of negativity.

Eventually, what you call the negative side of yourself can become the greatest force for renewal, creativity, and growth within you. Each one of us has this task. It is a wise person who knows where their negativity lies and yet does not become addicted to it. There is a greater and more generous presence behind your negativity. In its transfiguration, you move into the light that is hidden in this larger presence. To continually transfigure the faces of your own death ensures that, at the end of your life, your physical death will be no stranger, robbing you against your will of the life that you have had; you will know its face intimately. Since you have overcome your fear, your death will be a meeting with a life-long friend from the deepest side of your own nature.

Another face of death, another way it expresses itself in our daily experience, is through fear. There is no soul without the shadow of fear. It is a courageous person who is able to identify his fears and work with them as forces for creativity and growth. There are different levels of fear within each of us. One of the most powerful aspects of fear is its uncanny ability to falsify what is real in your life. There is no force I know that can so quickly destroy the happiness and tranquillity of life.

There are different levels of fear. Many people are terrified of letting go and use control as a mechanism to order and structure their lives. They like to be in control of what is happening around them and to them. But too much control is destructive. You become trapped in the protective program that you weave around your life. This can put you outside many of the blessings destined for you. Control must always remain partial and temporary. At times of pain, and particularly at the time of your death, you may not be able to maintain this control. Mystics have always recognized that to come deeper into the divine presence within, you need to practice detachment. When you begin to let go, it is amazing how enriched your life becomes. False things, which you have desperately held on to, move away very quickly from you. Then what is real, what you love deeply, and what really belongs to you comes deeper into you. Now no one can ever take them away from you.

DEATH AS THE ROOT OF FEAR

Some people are afraid of being themselves. Many people allow their lives to be limited by that fear. They play a continual game, fashioning a careful persona that they think the world will accept or admire. Even when they are in their solitude, they remain afraid of meeting themselves. One of the most sacred duties of one's destiny is the duty to be yourself. When you come to accept yourself and like yourself, you learn not to be afraid of your own nature. At that moment, you come into rhythm with your soul, and then you are on your own ground. You are sure and poised. You are balanced. It is so futile to weary your life with the politics of fashioning a persona in order to meet the expectations of other people. Life is very short, and we have a special destiny waiting to unfold for us. Sometimes through our fear of being ourselves, we sidestep that destiny and end up hungry and impoverished in a famine of our own making.

The best story I know about the presence of fear is an old story from India about a man condemned to spend the night in a cell with a poisonous snake. If he made the slightest movement, the snake would kill him. All night the man stood petrified in the corner of the cell, afraid even to breathe for fear of alerting the snake. As the first light of dawn reached into the cell, he could make out the shape of the snake in the other corner. He was deeply relieved not to have alerted it. Then as the light of dawn increased further and became really bright, he saw that it was not a snake but an old rope lying in the corner of the cell. The moral of the story suggests that there are harmless things, like that old rope, lying around in many of the rooms of our minds. Our anxiousness then works on them until we convert them into monsters that hold us imprisoned and petrified in small rooms in our lives.

One of the ways of transfiguring the power and presence of your death is to transfigure your fear. I find it very helpful when I am anxious or afraid to ask myself of what am I really afraid. This is a liberating question. Fear is like fog; it spreads everywhere and falsifies the shape of everything. When you pin it down to that one question, it shrinks back to a proportion that you are able to engage. When you know what is frightening you, you take back the power you had invested in fear. This also separates your fear from the night of the unknown, out of which every fear lives. Fear multiplies in anonymity; it shuns having a name. When you can name your fear, your fear begins to shrink.

All fear is rooted in the fear of death. There is a time or phase in every life when you are really terrified of dying. We live in time, and time is notoriously contingent. No one can say with certainty what is going to happen to us tonight, tomorrow, or next week. Time can bring anything to the door of your life. One of the terrifying aspects of life is this unpredictability. Anything can happen to you. Now as you are reading this, there are people all over the world who are being savagely visited by the unexpected. Things are, now, happening to them that will utterly disturb their lives forever. Their nest of belonging is broken, their lives will never be the same again. Someone in a doctor's office is receiving bad news; someone in a road accident will never walk again; someone's lover is leaving, never to return. When we look into the future of our lives, we cannot predict what will happen. We can be sure of nothing. Yet there is one fact that is certain, namely, that a time will come, a morning, an evening, or a night, when you will be called to make the journey out of this world, when you will have to die. Though that fact is certain, the nature of the fact remains completely contingent. In other words, you do not know where you will die, how you will die, when you will die, or who will be there or how you will feel. These facts about the nature of your death, the most decisive event in your life, remain completely opaque.

Though death is the most powerful and ultimate experience in one's life, our culture goes to great pains to deny its presence. In a certain sense, the whole world of media, image, and advertising is trying to cultivate a cult of immortality; consequently, the rhythm of death in life is rarely acknowledged.

As Emmanuel Levinas so poignantly states it,

My death comes from an instant upon which I can in no way exercise my power. I do not run up against an obstacle which at last I touch in that collision, which, in surmounting or enduring it, I integrate into my life, suspending its otherness. Death is a menace that approaches me as mystery, its secrecy determines it, or it approaches without being able to be assumed, such that the time that separates me from my death dwindles and dwindles without end, involves a sort of last interval which my consciousness cannot traverse, and where a leap will somehow be produced from death to me. The last part of the route will be crossed without me; the time of death flows upstream. . . .

DEATH IN THE CELTIC TRADITION

The Celtic tradition had a refined sense of the miracle of death. There are some beautiful prayers about death in Celtic spirituality. For the Celts, the eternal world was so close to the natural world that death was not seen as a terribly destructive or threatening event. When you enter the eternal world, you are going home to where no shadow, pain, or darkness can ever touch you again. There is a lovely Celtic prayer on this theme:

> I am going home with thee, to thy home, to thy home,
> I am going home with thee, to thy home of winter.
> I am going home with thee, to thy home, to thy home,
> I am going home with thee, to thy home of autumn of
>   spring and of summer.
> I am going home with thee, thy child of my love to thy
>   eternal bed to thy perpetual sleep.
>
> (TRANS. A. CARMICHAEL)

In that prayer the whole world of nature and the seasons is linked up beautifully with the presence of the eternal life.

You will never understand death or appreciate its loneliness until it visits. In Connemara the people say, *"Ni thuigfidh tú an bás go dtiocfaidh sé ag do dhorás féin"*—that is, "You will never understand death until it comes to your own door."

Another phrase they have is, *"Is fear díreach é an bás, ní chuire-ann sé scéal ar bith roimhe"*—that is, "Death is a very direct individual who sends no story before him." Another phrase is *"Ní féidir dul i bhfolach ar an mbás"*—that is, "There is no place to hide from death." This means that when death is searching for you, it will always know where to find you.

WHEN DEATH VISITS . . .

Death is a lonely visitor. After it visits your home, nothing is ever the same again. There is an empty place at the table; there is an absence in the house. Having someone close to you die is an incredibly strange and desolate experience. Something breaks within you then that will never come together again. Gone is the person whom you loved, whose face and hands and body you knew so well. This body, for the first time, is completely empty. This is very frightening and strange. After the death many questions come into your mind concerning where the person has gone, what they see and feel now. The death of a loved one is bitterly lonely. When you really love someone, you would be willing to die in their place. Yet no one can take another's place when that time comes. Each one of us has to go alone. It is so strange that when someone dies, they literally disappear. Human experience includes all kinds of continuity and discontinuity, closeness and distance. In death, experience reaches the ultimate

frontier. The deceased literally falls out of the visible world of form and presence. At birth you appear out of nowhere, at death you disappear to nowhere. If you have a row with someone you love and she goes away, and if you then desperately need to meet again, regardless of the distance, you can travel to where she is to find her. The terrible moment of loneliness in grief comes when you realize that you will never see the deceased again. The absence of their life, the absence of their voice, face, and presence become something that, as Sylvia Plath says, begins to grow beside you like a tree.

THE *CAOINEADH*: THE IRISH MOURNING TRADITION

One of the lovely things about the Irish tradition is its great hospitality to death. When someone in the village dies, everyone goes to the funeral. First everyone comes to the house to sympathize. All the neighbors gather around to support the family and to help them. It is a lovely gift. When you are really desperate and lonely, you need neighbors to help you, support you, and bring you through that broken time. In Ireland there was a tradition known as the *caoineadh*. These were people, women mainly, who came in and keened the deceased. It was a kind of high-pitched wailing cry full of incredible loneliness. The narrative of the *caoineadh* was actually the history of the person's life as these women had known him or her. A sad liturgy, beautifully woven of narrative, was gradually put into the place of the person's new absence from the world. The *caoineadh* gathered all the key events of the person's life. It was certainly heartbreakingly lonely, but it made a hospitable, ritual space for the mourning and sadness of the bereaved family. The *caoineadh* helped people to let the emotion of loneliness and grief flow in a natural way.

We have a tradition in Ireland known as the wake. This ensures that the person who has died is not left on their own the night after death. Neighbors, family members, and friends accompany the body through the early hours of its eternal change. Some drinks and tobacco are usually provided. Again, the conversation of the friends weaves a narrative of remembrance from the different elements of that person's life.

THE SOUL THAT KISSED THE BODY

It takes a good while to really die. For some people, it can be quick, yet the way the soul leaves the body is different for each individual. For some people, it may take a couple of days before the final withdrawal of soul is completed. There is a lovely anecdote from the Munster region about a man who had died. As the soul left the body, it went to the door of the house to begin its journey back to the eternal place. But the soul looked back at the now-empty body and lingered at the door. Then it went back and kissed the body and talked to it. The soul thanked the body for being such a hospitable place for its life journey and remembered the kindnesses the body had shown it during life.

In the Celtic tradition, there is a great sense that the dead do not live far away. In Ireland there are always places, fields, and old ruins where the ghosts of people were seen. That kind of folk memory recognizes that people who have lived in a place, even when they move to invisible form, somehow still remain attached to that place. There is also the tradition known as the *Coiste Bodhar,* or the Deaf Coach. Living in a little village on the side of a mountain, my aunt as a young woman heard that coach late one night. This was a small village of houses all close together. She was at home on her own, and she heard what sounded like barrels crashing against each other. This fairy coach came right down along the street beside her house and continued along a mountain path. All the dogs in the village heard the noise and followed the coach. The story suggests that the invisible world has secret pathways where funerals travel.

THE *BEAN SÍ*

In the Irish tradition, there is also a very interesting figure called the *Bean Sí*. *Sí* is another word for fairies, and *Bean Sí* is the word for Fairy Woman. This is a spirit who cries for someone who is about to die. My father heard her crying one evening. Two days later a neighbor, from a family for whom the *Bean Sí* always cried, died. In this, the Celtic Irish tradition recognizes that the eternal and the transient worlds are woven in and through each other. Very often at death, the inhabitants of the eternal world come out toward the visible world. It can take a person days or hours to die, and then often preceding the moment of death, that person might see their deceased mother, grandmother, grandfather, or some relation, spouse, or friend. When a person is close to death, the veil between this world and the eternal world is very thin. In some cases, the veil is actually removed for a moment so that you can indeed be given a glimpse into the eternal world. Your friends who now live in the eternal world come to meet you, to bring you home. Usually, for people who are dying to see their own friends gives them great strength, support, and encouragement. This elevated perception shows the incredible energy that surrounds the moment of death. The Irish tradition shows great hospitality to the possibilities of this moment. When a person dies, holy water is sprinkled in a circle around the person. This helps to keep dark forces away and to keep the presence of light with the newly dead as they go on their final journey.

Sometimes people are very worried about dying. There is no need to be afraid. When the moment of your dying comes, you will be given everything that you need to make that journey in a graceful, elegant, and trusting way.

A BEAUTIFUL DEATH

I was once present at the deathbed of a friend. She was a lovely young woman, a mother of two children. The priest who helped her to die was also a friend. He knew her soul and spirit. As it became apparent that she would die that night, she became frightened. He took her hand and prayed hard into his own heart, asking to receive the words to make a little bridge for her journey. He knew her life very deeply, so he began to unfold her memories. He told her of her goodness, beauty, and kindness. She was a woman who had never harmed anyone. She always helped everyone. He recalled the key events of her life. He told her there was no need for her to be afraid. She was going home, and there would be a welcome for her there. God, who had sent her here, would welcome her and embrace her and take her so gently and lovingly home. Of this, she could be completely assured. Gradually, an incredible serenity and calmness came over her. All of her panic was transfigured into a serenity that I have rarely met in this world. All her anxiousness, worry, and fear had completely vanished. Now she was totally in rhythm with herself, attuned and completely tranquil. He told her that she had to do the most difficult thing in her life. She had to say farewell to each member of her family. This was extremely lonely and difficult.

He went out and gathered her family. He told them that each of them could go in for five or ten minutes. They were to go in and talk to her, tell her how much they loved her and to tell her what she meant to them. They were not to cry or burden her. They could cry afterward, but now they were to concentrate completely on making her journey easy. Each one of them went in and talked to her, consoled her, and blessed her. Each of them came out shattered, but they had brought her the gifts of acknowledgment, recognition, and love, beautiful gifts to help her on her journey. She herself was wonderful. Then he went to her and anointed her with the holy oil, and we all said the prayers together. Smiling and serene, she went absolutely happily and beautifully on the journey that she had to make alone. It was a great privilege for me to be there. For the first time my own fear of death was transfigured. It showed me that if you live in this world with kindness, if you do not add to other people's burdens, but if you try to serve love, when the time comes for you to make the journey, you will receive a serenity, peace, and a welcoming freedom that will enable you to go to the other world with great elegance, grace, and acceptance.

It is an incredible privilege to be with someone who is making this journey into the eternal world. When you are present at the sacrament of someone's death, you should be very mindful of their situation. In other words, you should not concentrate so much on your own grief. You should rather strive to be fully present to, with, and for the person who is going on the journey. Everything should be done to completely facilitate the dying person, and to make the transition as easy and as comfortable as possible.

I love the Irish tradition of the wake. Its ritual affords the soul plenty of time to take its leave. The soul does not leave the body abruptly; this is a slow leave-taking. You will notice how the body changes in its first stages of death. The person does not really leave life for a while. It is very important not to leave the dead person on his own. Funeral homes are cold, clinical places. If at all possible, when the person dies, they should be left in their familiar surroundings so that they can make this deeper transition in a comfortable, easy, and secure way. The first few weeks after a person dies, that person's soul and memory should be minded and protected. One should say many prayers for the deceased to help the person make the journey home. Death is a threshold into the unknown, and everyone needs much shelter as they go on that journey.

Death is pushed to the margins in modern life. There is much drama about the funeral, but this often remains external and superficial. Our consumerist society has lost the sense of ritual and wisdom necessary to acknowledge this rite of passage. The person who has entered the voyage of death needs more in-depth care.

THE DEAD ARE OUR NEAREST NEIGHBORS

The dead are not far away; they are very, very near us. Each one of us someday will have to face our own appointment with death. I like to think of this as an encounter with your deepest nature and most hidden self. It is a journey toward a new horizon. As a child, when I looked up at the mountain near my village, I used to dream of the day when I would be old enough to go with my uncle up to the top of the mountain. I thought that I would be able to see the whole world on the horizon. I remember that I was very excited when the day finally came. My uncle was bringing sheep over the mountain, and he told me that I could come with him. As we climbed up the mountain and came to where I thought the horizon would be, it had disappeared. Not only was I not able to see everything when I got there, but another horizon was waiting, farther on. I was disappointed but also excited in an unfamiliar way. Each new level revealed a new world. Hans Georg Gadamer, a wonderful German philosopher, has a lovely phrase: "A horizon is something toward which we journey, but it is also something that journeys along with us." This is an illuminating metaphor for understanding the different horizons of your own growth. If you are striving to be equal to your destiny and worthy of the possibilities that sleep in the clay of your heart, then you should be regularly reaching new horizons. Against this perspective, death can be understood as the final horizon. Beyond there, the deepest well of your identity awaits you. In that well, you will behold the beauty and light of your eternal face.

THE EGO AND THE SOUL

In our struggle with the silent and secret companion, death, the crucial battle is the one between the ego and the soul. The ego is the defensive shell we pull around our lives. It is afraid; it is threatened and grasping. It acts in an overly protective way and is very competitive. The soul, on the other hand, has no barriers. As the great Greek philosopher Heraclitus said, "The soul has no limits." The soul is a pilgrim journeying toward endless horizons. There are no exclusion areas; the soul suffuses everything. Furthermore, the soul is in touch with the eternal dimension of time and is never afraid of what is yet to come. In a certain sense, the meeting with your own death in the daily forms of failure, pathos, negativity, fear, or destructiveness are actually opportunities to transfigure your ego. These are invitations to move out of that protective, controlling way of being toward an art of being that allows openness and hospitality. To practice this art of being is to come into your soul-rhythm. If you come into your soul-rhythm, then the final meeting with your physical death need not be threatening or destructive. That final meeting will be the encounter with your own deepest identity, namely, your soul.

Physical death, then, is not about the approach of a dark destructive monster that cuts off your life and drags you away to an unknown place. Masquerading behind the face of your physical death is the image and presence of your deepest self, which is waiting to meet and embrace you. Deep down, you hunger to meet your soul. All during the course of our lives we struggle to catch up with ourselves. We are so taken up, so busy and distracted, that we cannot dedicate enough time or recognition to the depths within us. We endeavor to see ourselves and meet ourselves; yet there is such complexity in us and so many layers to the human heart that we rarely ever encounter ourselves. The philosopher Husserl is very good on this subject. He talks about the *Ur-Präsenz*, the primal presence of a thing, an object, or a person. In our day-to-day experience, we can only glimpse the fullness of presence that is in us; we can never meet our own presence face-to-face. At our death, all the defensive barriers that separate and exclude us from our presence fall away; the full embrace of the soul gathers around us. For that reason, death need not be a negative or destructive event. Your death can be a wonderfully creative event opening you up to embrace the divine that always lived secretly inside you.

DEATH AS AN INVITATION TO FREEDOM

When you think about it, you should not let yourself be pressurized by life. You should never give away your power to a system or to other people. You should hold the poise, balance, and power of your soul within yourself. If no one can keep death away from you, then no one has ultimate power. All power is pretension. No one avoids death. Therefore, the world should never persuade you of its power over you, since it has no power whatever to keep death away from you. Yet it is within your own power to transfigure your fear of death. If you learn not to be afraid of your death, then you realize that you do not need to fear anything else either.

A glimpse at the face of your death can bring immense freedom to your life. It can make you aware of the urgency of the time you have here. The waste of time is one of the greatest areas of loss in life. So many people are, as Patrick Kavanagh put it, "preparing for life rather than living it." You only get one chance. You have one journey through life; you cannot repeat even one moment or retrace one footstep. It seems that we are meant to inhabit and live everything that comes toward us. In the underside of life there is the presence of our death. If you really live your life to the full, death will never have power over you. It will never seem like a destructive, negative event. It can become, for you, the moment of release into the deepest treasures of your own nature; it can be your full entry into the temple of your soul. If you are able to let go of things, you learn to die spiritually in little ways during your life. When you learn to let go of things, a greater generosity, openness, and breath comes into your life. Imagine this letting go multiplied a thousand times at the moment of your death. That release can bring you to a completely new divine belonging.

NOTHINGNESS: A FACE OF DEATH

Everything that we do in the world is bordered by nothingness. This nothingness is one of the ways that death appears to us. Nothingness is one of the faces of death. The life of the soul is about the transfiguration of nothingness. In a certain sense, nothing new can emerge if there is not a space for it. That empty space is the space that we called nothingness. R. D. Laing, the wonderful Scottish psychiatrist, used to say, "There is nothing to be afraid of." This means not only that there is no need to be afraid of anything, but also that there is nothing there to be afraid of, namely, that the nothingness is everywhere, all around us. Because we shrink from this terrain, emptiness and nothingness are undervalued. From a spiritual perspective, they can be recognized as modes of presence of the eternal. The eternal comes to us mainly in terms of nothingness and emptiness. Where there is no space, the eternal cannot awaken. Where there is no space, the soul cannot awaken. This is summed up beautifully in a wonderful poem by the Scottish poet Norman MacCaig:

PRESENTS

I give you an emptiness,
I give you a plenitude,
unwrap them carefully.

—one's as fragile as the other—
and when you thank me
I'll pretend not to notice the doubt in your voice
when you say they're just what you wanted.

Put them on the table by your bed.
When you wake in the morning
they'll have gone through the door of sleep
into your head. Wherever you go
they'll go with you and
wherever you are you'll wonder,
smiling about the fullness
you can't add to and the emptiness
that you can fill.

This beautiful poem suggests the dual rhythm of emptiness and plenitude at the heart of the life of the soul. Nothingness is the sister of possibility. It makes an urgent space for that which is new, surprising, and unexpected. When you feel nothingness and emptiness gnawing at your life, there is no need to despair. This is a call from your soul, awakening your life to new possibilities. It is also a sign that your soul longs to transfigure the nothingness of your death into the fullness of a life eternal, which no death can ever touch.

Death is not the end; it is a rebirth. Our presence in the

world is so poignant. The little band of brightness that we call our life is poised between the darkness of two unknowns. There is the darkness of the unknown at our origin. We suddenly emerged from this unknown, and the band of brightness called life began. Then there is the darkness at the end when we disappear again back into the unknown. Samuel Beckett is a wonderful writer who has meditated deeply on the mystery of death. His little play *Breath* is only a few minutes long. First, there is the birth cry, then a little breathing, and finally, the sigh of death. This drama synopsizes what happens in our lives. All of Beckett's works, especially *Waiting for Godot,* are about death. In other words, because death exists, time is radically relativized. All we do here is invent games to pass the time.

WAITING AND ABSENCE

A friend of mine was telling me a story about a neighbor. The children from the local school were going into town to see *Waiting for Godot.* This man took a ride on their bus. He intended to meet some of his drinking colleagues in town. He traveled in with the schoolchildren to the theater and went immediately to the two or three pubs where he thought his friends would be; but they were not there. Since he had no money, he ended up having to watch *Waiting for Godot.* He was describing the experience to my friend: "It was the strangest play I ever saw in my life; seemingly the fellow who was to play the main part never turned up, and the actors were forced to improvise all night."

I thought that was a good analysis of *Waiting for Godot*. I think it was the kind of review with which Samuel Beckett himself would have been very pleased. In a certain sense, we are always waiting for the great moment of gathering or belonging, and it always evades us. We are haunted with a deep sense of absence. There is something missing from our lives. We always expect it to be filled by a definite person, object, or project. We are desperate to fill this emptiness, but the soul tells us, if we listen to it, that this absence can never be filled.

Death is the great wound in the universe and the great wound in each life. Yet, ironically, this is the very wound that can lead to new spiritual growth. Thinking of your death can help you to radically alter your fixed and habitual perception. Instead of living according to the merely visible material realm of life, you begin to refine your sensibility and become aware of the treasures that are hidden in the invisible side of your life. A person who is really spiritual has developed a sense of the depth of his or her own invisible nature. Your invisible nature holds qualities and treasures that time can never damage. They belong absolutely to you. You do not need to grasp them, earn them, or protect them. These treasures are yours; no one else can ever take them from you.

BIRTH AS DEATH

Imagine if you could talk to a baby in the womb and explain its unity with the mother. How this cord of belonging gives it life. If you could then tell the baby that this was about to end. It was going to be expelled from the womb, pushed through a very narrow passage finally to be dropped out into vacant, open light. The cord that held it to this mother-womb was going to be cut, and it was going to be on its own forever more. If the baby could talk back, it would fear that it was going to die. For the baby within the womb, being born would seem like death. Our difficulty with these great questions is that we are only able to see them from one side. In other words, we can only see death from one side. Many have had the experience, but nobody has come back to tell us about it. Those who have died stay away; they do not return. Therefore, we cannot actually see the other half of the circle that death opens. Wittgenstein summed it up very nicely when he said, "Death is not an experience in one's life." It cannot be an experience because it is the end of the life in which and through which all experience came to you.

I like to imagine that death is about rebirth. The soul is now free in a new world where there is no more separation or shadow or tears. A friend of mine lost a son who was twenty-six years of age. I was at the funeral. Her other children were all there as the coffin was lowered into the grave. A terrible wail of sadness rose up from the brothers and sisters. She put her arms around them and said, *"Nà bigí ag caoineadh, níl tada dhó thios ansin ach amháin an clúdach a bhí air"*—that is, "Let ye not be crying because there is nothing of him down there, only the covering that was on him in this life." It is a lovely thought, a recognition that the body was merely covering and the soul is now freed for the eternal.

DEATH TRANSFIGURES OUR SEPARATION

In Connemara the graveyards are near the ocean, where there is a lot of sandy soil. To open the grave, the sod is cut on three sides. It is rolled back very carefully from the surface of the field, but it is not broken off. Then the coffin is put down. The prayers are said and the grave is blessed and filled. Then the sod is rolled out over the grave so that it fits exactly over the opening. A friend of mine calls it a "cesarean section in reverse." It is as if the womb of the earth, without being broken, is receiving back the individual who once left as a clay shape to live in separation above in the world. It is an image of homecoming, of being taken back completely again.

It is a strange and magical fact to be here, walking around in a body, to have a whole world within you and a world at your fingertips outside you. It is an immense privilege, and it is incredible that humans manage to forget the miracle of being here. Rilke said, "Being here is so much." It is uncanny how social reality can deaden and numb us so that the mystical wonder of our lives goes totally unnoticed. We are here. We are wildly and dangerously free. The more lonely side of being here is our separation in the world. When you live in a body you are separate from every other object and person. Many of our attempts to pray, to love, and to create are secret attempts at transfiguring that separation in order to build bridges outward so that others can reach us and we can reach them. At death, this physical separation is broken. The soul is released from its particular and exclusive location in this body. The soul then comes in to a free and fluent universe of spiritual belonging.

ARE SPACE AND TIME DIFFERENT IN THE ETERNAL WORLD?

Space and time are the foundation of human identity and perception. We never have a perception that does not have each of these elements in it. The element of space means that we are always in a state of separation. I am here. You are there. Even the person that you are closest to, the one you love, is still a separate world from you. That is the poignancy of love. Two people become so close that they really want to become one; but their separate spaces keep the distance between them. In space, we are always separated. The other component of perception and identity is time. Time always separates us, too. Time is primarily linear, disjointed, and fragmented. All of your past days have disappeared; they have vanished. The future has not come to you yet. All you have is the little stepping-stone of the present moment.

When the soul leaves the body, it is no longer under the burden and control of space and time. The soul is free; distance and separation hinder it no more. The dead are our nearest neighbors; they are all around us. Meister Eckhart was once asked, Where does the soul of a person go when the person dies? He said, no place. Where else would the soul be going? Where else is the eternal world? It can be nowhere other than here. We have falsely spatialized the eternal world. We have driven the eternal out into some kind of distant galaxy. Yet the eternal world does not seem to be a place but rather a different state of being. The soul of the person goes no place because there is no place else to go. This suggests that the dead are here with us, in the air that we are moving through all the time. The only difference between us and the dead is that they are now in an invisible form. You cannot see them with the human eye. But you can sense the presence of those you love who have died. With the refinement of your soul, you can sense them. You feel that they are near.

My father used to tell us a story about a neighbor who was very friendly with the local priest. There is a whole mythology in Ireland about druids and priests having special power. But this man and the priest used to go for long walks.

One day the man said to the priest, Where are the dead? The priest told him not to ask him questions like that. But the man persisted, and finally, the priest said, I will show you; but you are never to tell anyone. Needless to say, the man did not keep his word. The priest raised his right hand; the man looked out under the raised right hand and saw the souls of the departed everywhere all around as thick as the dew on blades of grass. Often our loneliness and isolation are the result of a failure of spiritual imagination. We forget that there is no such thing as empty space. All space is full of presence, particularly the presence of those who are now in eternal, invisible form.

For those who have died, the world of time is also different. Here we are caught in linear time. We have forgotten the past; it is lost to us. We cannot know the future. Time must be totally different for the dead because they live now within a circle of eternity. Earlier we talked about landscape and how the Irish landscape resisted linearity. How the Celtic mind never liked the line but always loved the shape of the circle. Within the circle, beginning and ending are sisters, and they belong within the shelter which the eternal offers of the unity of the year and the earth. I imagine that in the eternal world time has become the circle of eternity. Maybe when a person goes into that world, he or she can look back at what we call past time here. That person may also see all of future time. For the dead, present time is total presence. This suggests that our friends among the dead know us better than they can ever have known us in life. They know everything about us, even things that may disappoint them. But since they are now transfigured, their understanding and compassion are proportionate to everything they have come to know about us.

THE DEAD BLESS US

I believe that our friends among the dead really mind us and look out for us. Often there might be a big boulder of misery over your path about to fall on you, but your friends among the dead hold it back until you have passed by. One of the exciting developments that may happen in evolution and in human consciousness in the next several hundred years is a whole new relationship with the invisible, eternal world. We might begin to link up in a very creative way with our friends in the invisible world. We do not need to grieve for the dead. Why should we grieve for them? They are now in a place where there is no more shadow, darkness, loneliness, isolation, or pain. They are home. They are with God from whom they came. They have returned to the nest of their identity within the great circle of God. God is the greatest circle of all, the largest embrace in the universe, which holds visible and invisible, temporal and eternal, as one.

There are lovely stories in the Irish tradition of people dying and then meeting all their old friends. This is expressed powerfully in a wonderful novel by Mairtin Ó Cadhain called *Cré na Cille.* This is about life in a graveyard and all that is happening among the people buried there. In the eternal world, all is one. In spiritual space there is no distance. In eternal time there is no segmentation into today, yesterday, or tomorrow. In eternal time all is now; time is presence. I believe that this is what eternal life means: It is a life where all that we seek—goodness, unity, beauty, truth, and love—are no longer distant from us but are now completely present with us. There is a lovely poem by R. S. Thomas on the notion of eternity. It is deliberately minimal in form but very powerful:

> I think that maybe
> I will be a little surer
> of being a little nearer.
> That's all. Eternity
> is in the understanding
> that that little is more than enough.

Kahlil Gibran articulates how the unity in friendship that we call *anam ċara* overcomes even death:

> You were born together, and together you shall be for evermore. You shall be together when the white wings of death scatter your days. Aye, you shall be together even in the silent memory of God.

I would like to end this chapter with a lovely prayer-poem from thirteenth-century Persia.

Some nights stay up 'til dawn as the moon sometimes does
    for the sun.
Be a full bucket, pulled up the dark way of a well then
    lifted out into light.
Something opens our wings, something makes boredom
    and hurt disappear.
Someone fills the cup in front of us, we taste only
    sacredness.

A Blessing for Death

*I pray that you will have the blessing of being consoled and
    sure about your own death.*
May you know in your soul that there is no need to be afraid.
*When your time comes, may you be given every blessing and
    shelter that you need.*
*May there be a beautiful welcome for you in the home that
    you are going to.*
*You are not going somewhere strange. You are going back to
    the home that you never left.*
*May you have a wonderful urgency to live your life to the
    full.*

May you live compassionately and creatively and transfigure
  everything that is negative within you and about you.
When you come to die may it be after a long life.
May you be peaceful and happy and in the presence of those
  who really care for you.
May your going be sheltered and your welcome assured.
May your soul smile in the embrace of your anam ċara.

FURTHER RECOMMENDED READING

Adorno, Theodor W. *Minima Moralia.* Frankfurt, 1989.

Aristotle. *De Anima.* London, 1986.

———. *Ethics.* London, 1986.

Augustine. *The Confessions.* London, 1945.

Bachelard, Gaston. *The Poetics of Space.* Boston, 1969.

Baudrillard, Jean. *Fatal Strategies.* New York, 1990.

Berger, John. *Ways of Seeing.* London, 1981.

Bradley, Ian. *The Celtic Way.* London, 1993.

Cardenal, Marie. *The Words to Say It.* London, 1983.

Carmichael, Alexander. *Carmina Gadelica.* Edinburgh, 1994.

Curtis, P. J. *Notes from the Heart: A Celebration of Traditional Irish Music.* Dublin, 1994.

Dillard, Annie. *The Writing Life.* New York, 1989.

Kennelly, Brendan, ed. *The Penguin Book of Irish Verse.* London, 1970.

Kinsella, Thomas, trans. *The Taín.* Oxford, 1986.

Levertov, Denise. *The Poet in the World.* New York, 1973.

Levinas, Emmanuel. *Totality and Infinity.* Pittsburgh.

Low, Mary. *Celtic Christianity and Nature.* Edinburgh, 1996.

Matthews, Caitlín. *Celtic Blessings.* Dorset, 1994.

Merleau Ponty, M. *Phenomenology of Perception.* London, 1981.

Moriarty, John. *Dreamtime.* Dublin, 1994.

Murdoch, Iris. *Metaphysics as a Guide to Morals.* London, 1992.

Murphy, Gerard. *Early Irish Lyrics.* Oxford, 1956.

Murray, P., ed. *The Deer's Cry: A Treasury of Irish Religious Verse.* Dublin, 1986.

O'Céirín, Kit and Cyril. *Women of Ireland.* Tir Eolas, 1996.

O'Donoghue, Noel Dermot. *The Mountain behind the Mountain: Aspects of the Celtic Tradition.* Edinburgh, 1993.

O'Donohue, John. *Person als Vermittlung: Die Dialektik von Individualität und Allgemeinheit in Hegels Phänomenologie des Geistes. Eine philosophisch-Theologische Interpretation.* Mainz, 1993.

O h-Ogain, Daithi. *Myth, Legend and Romance: An Encyclopaedia of the Irish Folk Tradition.* New York, 1991.

Plotinus. *The Ennead,* trans. Stephen MacKenna. London, 1996.

Rahner, Karl. *Foundations of Christian Faith: An Introduction to the Idea of Christianity.* London, 1978.

Sells, Michael A. *Mystical Languages of Unsaying.* Chicago, 1994.

Sheldrake, Rupert. *The Rebirth of Nature.* London, 1990.

Smith, Cyprian. *The Way of Paradox: Spiritual Life as Taught by Meister Eckhart.* London, 1987.

Steiner, George. *Real Presences.* London, 1989.

Waddel, Helen. *The Desert Fathers.* London, 1962.

Whyte, David. *The Heart Aroused.* New York, 1995.